D0984340

CONGRESS
IN ACTION

CONGRESS IN ACTION

The Environmental Education Act

DENNIS W. BREZINA

AND

ALLEN OVERMYER

Foreword by
SENATOR GAYLORD NELSON

Afterword by
CONGRESSMAN JOHN BRADEMAS

The Free Press
A Division of Macmillan Publishing Co., Inc.
NEW YORK

Collier Macmillan Publishers
LONDON

THE FREE PRESS
A DIVISION OF MACMILLAN PUBLISHING CO., INC.
866 THIRD AVENUE, NEW YORK, N.Y. 10022

COLLIER-MACMILLAN CANADA LTD.

LIBRARY OF CONGRESS CATALOG CARD NUMBER: 73-6492

PRINTED IN THE UNITED STATES OF AMERICA

PRINTING NUMBER

1   2   3   4   5   6   7   8   9   10

Library of Congress Cataloging in Publication Data

Brezina, Dennis, 1937-
    Congress in action: the Environmental education
act.

    "Environmental education act": p.
    Includes bibliographical references.
    1. United States. Laws, statutes, etc. Environ-
mental education act. 2. United States. Congress.
3. Environmental policy--United States. I. Overmyer,
Allen, 1940-   joint author. II. United States.
Laws, statutes, etc. Environmental education act.
1974. III. Title.
KF3775.A323A163   344'.73'046   73-6492
ISBN 0-02-904900-8

250996

To
Byron and Brent
and
Mother and Father

Contents

vii

Foreword

THE FIRST Earth Day was a remarkable event that changed the politics of the country. On that day—April 22, 1970—a new issue was born that is here to stay.

Earth Day was proposed as a means of making the environmental issue part of the nation's political dialogue, and its success helped to ensure that the cause of environmental quality would be a matter that leaders at every level of public life would have to take into consideration.

Grass-roots conservationists and ecologists began forming powerful political coalitions that presented forces of unity demanding environmental awareness and consideration. Politicians soon learned that environmental indifference could be politically hazardous.

All this was necessary. The political arena is where the problems are solved. Earth Day gave the environmental movement the political clout it needed, and the environmentalists no longer were talking only to each other. Now others are listening.

Earth Week is now observed on an annual basis as a continuing reminder that restoring and protecting the environment will require an unwavering effort on the part of citizens and institutions, public and private. That effort will not end because significant improvements have been made in the past few years. Restoring, preserving, and protecting the environment will continue for decades because the quality of life in an ever expanding society is always in danger.

Ultimately, the ability to reverse our abuse of the environment will depend upon whether or not we can change our style of life. The best way to do that is through long-term, sustained educational efforts. The environmental issue is not a temporary fad or a fashionable issue. It is an issue that is too important not to be sustained, and that is why the Environmental Education Act was created.

That Act attempts to perpetuate the spirit of Earth Day in that every man is responsible for the environment of this world. It recognizes that sound environmental principles must be taught and incorporated into every facet of our daily life if we are to preserve a liveable planet for future generations.

In order to achieve that goal we are going to have to adopt new policies that build environmental considerations into the daily business of the nation.

The first must involve adopting a new attitude of respect for ourselves as a species and for all other living creatures. We must accept the fact that the earth is a finite system incapable of being endlessly exploited, a relatively insignificant particle in a tremendous galaxy, with a thin envelope of air and a much thinner coating of soil, with limited water and minerals—and with a limited capacity to support life.

We must recognize that when we upset the balance of nature, we set off a chain reaction that ultimately affects all living things, including ourselves. We threaten the survival of other species and in doing so seal our own fate.

As in the lines of the poet John Donne: "And therefore never send to know for whom the bell tolls; it tolls for thee."

Gaylord Nelson
United States Senator
January 1973

Preface

THIS BOOK is the work of two former congressional staff
members who believe that a book of substance about Congress can be written by people not in the academic world.
Our credentials consist primarily of knowledge and practical insights gained through direct observation and participation in the congressional process over a prolonged
period of time. We make no prentense of implying that this
work is definitive or encyclopedic or that it will serve as a
paradigm for future writers on Congress. However, the
authors feel strongly that few scholars of Congress have
exhibited in their writings a good "feel" for that institution
as it actually operates.

We have tried to write a book about a living, dynamic
institution. The setting, the present, is that of a dawning
postwar period in which the legislative branch historically
would be expected to regain much of the power it ordinarily loses during a major war. It is our hope that new and
refreshing approaches—systematic but not scientific—will
be undertaken when Congress is analyzed and written
about, so that student, teacher, and layman will have a
better understanding of the most democratic body in the
federal government.

No book of this nature can be satisfactorily completed
without the assistance and guidance of many people. We

are deeply indebted to those who helped not only to make this book possible but to make the Environmental Education Act a reality: George E. Lowe, Sylvia Wright, Paul Cromwell, and other members of the Office of Environmental Education in the Office of Education were most resourceful in both substance and moral support. Logan H. Salada, Jr., special assistant to the late former Commissioner of Education, James E. Allen, Jr., was helpful in providing policy-level information about the Executive Branch, which, we hope, has given this book more balance and a higher degree of veracity.

On Capitol Hill numerous staff aides were genuinely concerned about the success of our endeavors. They include Jack Duncan and Ronald Katz of the parent-education subcommittee on the House side; Stephen Wexler and Richard D. Smith of the education subcommittee in the Senate; Harley M. Dirks of the Senate Appropriations Committee; E. Winslow Turner of the Senate Government Operations Committee; and, most importantly, Congressman John Brademas and Senator Gaylord Nelson, who took an encouraging interest in the work.

Many others were extremely helpful, but none more than Abby Brezina and Jan Eidsness, who shouldered the burden of typing the manuscript and who exhibited the patience of Job while two bleary-eyed authors-to-be rewrote and haggled over every line of every chapter. Credit is due Bruce Lederer, our friendly research assistant, whose efforts were timely and valuable. Finally, we owe a great debt to David C. Harrop, formerly with the Free Press, who was our good angel, and to David McDermott and Ellen Simon of that organization with whom we have subsequently wor⌐ ⌐.

The authors accept the responsibility for any error in

fact or perception of fact that may appear in the book. We are grateful for the unselfish help of those who checked the manuscript, which has given us confidence that our apologies will be few.

We welcome comment and criticism on our interpretation of Congress because we believe—and this is one of the major purposes of the book—that there is no single approach to understanding how the political process works at the federal level of *our* government.

The book contains no source footnotes because the documents referred to are largely records of congressional hearings, which are not normally a part of the collection of major libraries and are also out of print, and memoranda of limited distribution. The reader would find it impossible to look up most of the references in an average library. Moreover, the book was designed intentionally not to be a work "replete" with footnotes.

The preponderance of the quoted passages is contained in published hearings of Congress. During the legislative phase, the hearings took place before the Select Subcommittee on Education, Committee on Labor and Education, U.S. House of Representatives and the Subcommittee on Education of the Committee on Labor and Public Welfare, U.S. Senate.

The House and Senate Appropriations committees were the bodies of Congress that held hearings on funding for the Environmental Education Act.

The activities of three committees are referred to in the chapter on oversight. The first set of hearings was held by the Senate Subcommittee on Intergovernmental Relations, Committee on Government Operations. The second was held by the Senate Special Subcommittee on Human Resources, Committee on Labor and Public Welfare. The third was held by the House Select Subcommittee on Education, Committee on Labor and Education.

The epilogue refers to a final oversight hearing that the same House subcommittee initiated in April 1972.

The remainder of the quotes come from government memoranda, speeches, newspapers, and the Congressional Record.

Dennis W. Brezina
and
Allen Overmyer

Introduction

THIS IS a book about Congress in action. It is a case study that follows the course of a particular bill, the Environmental Education Act, from its grass roots beginnings in the environmental movement through the total legislative cycle and into its implementation as a program in the federal government.

The book deals with the three main functions of Congress—legislation, appropriations, and oversight—as they relate to the Environmental Education Act. Its scope extends beyond the legislative process itself, which ends with enactment into law and the President's signature. It encompasses the ensuing battle over appropriations and the exercise of the congressional oversight role to ensure that the program created by the Act would be carried out. The book points out the importance for Congress to follow through on its legislative initiatives, and it illustrates the continuing nature of the attempt to translate legislative ideas into reality.

The bill's progress toward implementation necessarily involved a sustained interaction between the Legislative and Executive Branches, which was directly related to two of the basic doctrinal issues of American government: checks and balances and the separation of powers. The question of checks and balances is manifested in an institutional context at its most fundamental level, which is the point of confrontation between congressmen and administrators before congressional subcommittees, where each represents the positions and perspectives of his own branch of government.

The focus of this work is on Congress, and the actions and events surrounding the bill's history are seen *primarily* from a congressional viewpoint. This viewpoint is balanced with a presentation of Executive Branch activities and perspectives as they relate to the legislation, but the degree of emphasis and detail about congressional activities is greater. The interaction between the branches is largely based upon two differing perceptions. To congressmen who sponsored the legislation, it appeared that a program they had authorized might be delayed and resisted by the Executive Branch. From the Executive Branch's point of view, the bill initially was not essential, but they did not strongly oppose it. Later, when the bill was amended, the Executive Branch actively fought the measure because it appeared that Congress was specifying details of administration that should normally be left to the Executive.

As a case study of a single bill progressing through the three major processes of the Legislative Branch, the book is horizontal in nature—covering all stages of the bill's progress—rather than vertical—dwelling in depth on a particular phase of the congressional process. Similar studies have often addressed only a single legislative function.

The book attempts to involve the reader in the dynamics of the congressional process, giving him a feeling for what actually happens in the enactment and implementation of legislation. The approach is empirical rather than theoretical, and generalizations are derived only from occurrences directly affecting this bill.

The narrative is presented chronologically as a series of steps through which the Act progressed. It is made clear that at many of these steps the progress could have been severely delayed or halted altogether. Therefore, pitfalls are often discussed as they were perceived, whether or not they actually materialized. In actuality, the bill sailed through Congress in a very short time for a new legislative initiative, possibly giving to some the impression that Congress would not follow through in its efforts to ensure implementation. Twelve months after the bill was introduced it had become public law and had received its first appropriation. Yet after another full year the congressional sponsors felt that the Act was not being implemented as they intended, and oversight hearings were initiated to help ensure the continued progress.

The creation of a legislative reality reaffirms the well-worn adage that politics is an art and not a science. The rules and procedures are guidelines only, and within the guidelines there is wide latitude for flexibility and maneuver. The art of legislating depends upon people, timing, and events; personalities, luck, and know-how are as important as the rules. Legislative strategy concerning all three functions calls for compromise, trade-offs, and timing. These are not the necessary evils of the political system, but rather the basic and legitimate principles by which it operates

The total process of producing effective legislation is analogous to rolling the stone of Sisyphus to the top of the hill. In Greek mythology Sisyphus was condemned to the eternal punishment of pushing a great boulder to the top of a hill and then having it roll immediately to the bottom, with the process repeated endlessly. Similarly, the legislative process is seemingly never finished. As soon as one victory is won another task appears, and then another. The proper role of the legislator is to keep the bill and later the program moving forward by trying to act at the exact time and with the exact force needed to sustain its progress, however prolonged the effort might be.

CONGRESS
IN ACTION

1

Confrontation: Executive and Legislative

BRADEMAS: I do not know as I sit here now, if there presently exists an Office of Environmental Education, and in light of your testimony . . . I do not see how anyone can be sure. What is the fact? Does it exist, will it exist, was it born in the summer, where is it?

MARLAND: I will try again, and I use the word "office" perhaps loosely.

BRADEMAS: Do not use it loosely. Have you read the law?

MARLAND: . . . It was a program, and it remains a program to this day, until the papers are completed, moving this program into the office of development . . . and these papers are now in process, Mr. Chairman.

BRADEMAS: There does not now exist an Office of Environmental Education?

MARLAND: Not in the formal sense. There is a func-

tioning operation in the Office of Education which
I have loosely and perhaps erroneously described
as the Office of Environmental Education, and, if
so, I apologize for misleading the Committee.

The apology was from U.S. Commissioner of Education
Sidney P. Marland, Jr., in testimony before a House subcommittee chaired by Representative John Brademas of
Indiana. The subcommittee was holding oversight hearings to find out what had happened to legislation Congress
had enacted one year earlier creating a new kind of educational program and an administrative office to run it. The
question was: Where was the program and where was the
office?

Commissioner Marland was apologizing because he had
referred to a loosely structured program as a formal office.
Marland's admission that the office had not been officially
designated contradicted his statement earlier in the testimony that it already existed and climaxed what the legislators saw as a yearlong series of efforts by the Executive
Branch to avoid carrying out the intent of Congress and
the law of the United States.

The law was the Environmental Education Act, initiated
and passed by Congress and signed by President Nixon on
October 30, 1970. It was an educational response to the
growing awareness of the environmental quality crisis, and
its purpose was to incorporate environmental learning into
the American system of education. Besides the administrative office, the legislation also established an advisory council to provide policy guidance for the program. After a
year had passed, the administrative machinery still had not
been assembled, despite repeated assurances from the
Office of Education that the necessary steps would be com-

pleted in the "near future." Brademas, who authored the bill, felt that the program was in danger of being buried, either by design or through bureaucratic foot-dragging, or a combination of the two, and he was using sledgehammer tactics against the Office of Education to prevent this from happening.

The legislation stated that an Office of Environmental Education would be created directly under the Commissioner to ensure it a high-priority status. Marland said the office had been established "by administrative order" two months earlier. Brademas bore down on the Commissioner's use of the term "office." The Commissioner insisted that there was no difference between a program and an office and that the problem was one of semantics.

To Brademas an important legal distinction was involved. An office would be a formal structure with the Environmental Education Act (Public Law 91-516) as its statutory base, and, once officially created, it could not be modified without congressional action. Congress would be able to maintain direct accountability over it, whereas a program would depend for its continued existence upon the will of the Office of Education and could be shifted and modified at the discretion of the Office.

The question here was one of trust. Brademas did not believe the Executive Branch intended to carry out the law.

He said:

> All we want you in the Office of Education to do is obey the law, and if you look at this statute, Public Law 91–516 . . . you will see Section 3 (2) (1), "There is established within the Office of Education an Office of Environment Education." . . . All we want you to

> do is keep your word and do what the Congress said
> to do.

Representative Ogden Reid (D –N.Y.) pressed Dr. Marland further for a commitment to establish the office within two weeks:

> Could I make the request, and get your concurrence
> on the record, and your commitment on the record,
> that the Office will be formally established in November?

The Commissioner replied, "Yes. The answer is a firm yes."

The day after the hearings took place the Office of Education issued a press release announcing that an Office of Environmental Education was being created on that day.

A second point on which Brademas said the Executive Branch had not obeyed the law was in the mandatory appointment of the Advisory Council. This was a step to be taken before projects were funded or other major commitments made.

There was no Advisory Council in existence before the hearings took place, although one had been in the process of selection since shortly after the bill was passed. The first announcement of its appointment came during the hearings. In answer to questioning from Brademas, Marland made public a list of the initial 18 members selected for the council and gave the date for its first meeting. It was apparent that the timing of the announcement had been prompted by the hearings. The names had not yet been cleared through all the necessary channels. Brademas said he was "reliably advised" that the meeting date was set only after the subcommittee hearings had been scheduled.

This confrontation between the legislative and executive branches ended with a declaration from Brademas that the subcommittee would probably want to take the very unusual step of calling the Commissioner back in a few weeks "just to see how things have been coming along." Brademas said he had observed in the legislative process "enormous gaps between what is said and what is done," and his subcommittee had particular responsibility to "tend to the children which it has nurtured, legislatively, so that they grow up strong and healthy, and are not strangled in their cribs . . ."

Through the oversight hearings on the Environmental Education Act, Congress was exercising one of its three major functions, which are legislation, appropriation, and oversight. The legislative process is the cycle of passing a bill through Congress, from initiation to enactment. The appropriations process is a similar step, providing funds to carry out the legislated activity. The third step, utilized much less frequently than the others, is in this instance an attempt to watch over the results of the first two. It is a means of assuring that any administration properly and effectively carries out the law.

The confrontation between the two branches was the culmination of a prolonged uphill battle on the part of Congress to bring a program into existence. The congressional task of making laws, from idea to reality, is a continuous one, and it involves repeated interaction between the executive and legislative branches. With the Executive Branch reacting to a legislative mandate and Congress attempting to ensure that the mandate was followed, it also exemplifies the system of checks and balances at its most direct and fundamental level.

THE ENVIRONMENTAL EDUCATION ACT

Although the Environmental Education Act was relatively unknown and called for a minuscule authorization level by federal standards, it was a controversial act, and the activities surrounding its passage and implementation focused directly on some of the major concepts related to the American system of government. Its history was a model of the three main congressional functions and a microcosm of institutional interaction at the federal level.

When it was passed, the law was a "sleeper." The authorization level for its first year of operation was only $5 million, or 1/1,000 of the annual budget for the Office of Education. The act had a potential impact much out of keeping with funds made available for it because it was designed to reach out beyond the education establishment to touch as great a number of people as possible with a small amount of money.

Environmental education was envisioned as both a new subject area (the environment) and a new approach to learning. It aimed at increasing one's awareness and understanding of his environment by using the natural and man-made world as a source of teaching material. It removed a major barrier between the student and the world around him and taught him to relate to the world directly rather than to someone's interpretation of it in a textbook. It was oriented toward processes and problem solving, and its approach was holistic, encompassing all disciplines and stressing the interrelatedness of problems of the environment to people. In its broad approach environmental education contradicts the modern Western educational tradition of dividing learning into separate disciplines. It is a unifying and thus a reform concept.

Its direct antecedents were in the British open-classroom methods that were introduced in the United States during the 1960s. The open-classroom concept deformalizes the schoolroom and the teaching process, encouraging children to learn by following their own curiosity. The teacher acts as a guide to the student's own discovery process, and the student frequently acts as a teacher. The children are freer to choose their own activities and to explore the community or environment around them, breaking down the artificiality of the classroom world. With environmental education the community becomes the classroom, and the man-made world and the world of nature are integrated into the learning process.

The Environmental Education Act represented an attempt to translate the idea of environmental learning into a public policy along with an operational federal program. Its purpose, as stated in the Act, was "to establish education programs to encourage understanding of policies, and support of activities, designed to enhance environmental quality and maintain ecological balance." It provided grants for a wide range of activities at all educational levels, from kindergarten to adult education. These included encouraging the development of new environmental curricula; establishing school programs; training teachers, government employees, community and business leaders; providing for community-education programs; and aiding mass-media efforts concerning the environment and ecology.

Despite its limited authorization the bill's potential impact was great for several reasons. First, the money would be divided into relatively small grants that would fund a large number of programs. Secondly, the programs would be designed to involve as many people as possible in communities, educational institutions, government, and industry. With a high ratio of people to federal dollars a small amount of money would go a long way. Also, the funds were not to be used to conduct programs on a continuing basis but to experiment and develop pilot processes that could be applied on a broader scale. Further, the bill contained a section providing for "technical assistance" to be given other education agencies, private nonprofit organizations, and elements of government at all levels to carry out programs related to environmental quality and ecological balance. Finally, because it envisioned that other programs of the Office of Education would fund projects in which all subjects are interrelated and traditional barriers between disciplines would be broken down, potentially the bill had broad implications for restructuring American education.

The Stone of Sisyphus

The process of bringing a federal program into existence, from conception of a legislative idea through passage and translation into action, is like Sisyphus' eternal struggle to roll his great stone to the top of that hill in the infernal regions of Greek mythology. No sooner does the stone reach the top that it goes crashing back downhill, and the cycle must begin again. Like the labor of Sisyphus the path of legislation from idea to reality is a series of seemingly endless steps in which each small victory is followed by another challenge presenting new dangers and new decisions.

The first step is the legislative cycle, which begins with introduction of the bill and follows a roughly parallel course through both houses—in subcommittee and committee action, floor votes and conference—and ends with final passage and the presidential signature. At this point the bill becomes public law. If the bill authorizes funding for a new program, the law is meaningless unless the next step, the appropriation process, is taken. The appropriations cycle generally duplicates the authorization procedure, with similar pitfalls. Legislation already signed into law frequently dies because the appropriations process is not completed.

A good example of a law that died from lack of funds is the International Education Act, which was enacted in 1966 to provide federal support for students from other countries to study and conduct research at universities in the United States. Congress never appropriated the funds authorized in the bill, and no such program came into existence. Its years of authorization passed, and the law was dead. John Brademas was the author of this bill, and he was deeply conscious of its fate during the passage of the Environmental Education Act.

Even completion of the appropriations process does not ensure that a legislative program will exist as envisioned. It is up to the Executive Branch to carry out the congressional mandate in the implementation phase. There are many reasons why the Executive Branch under any administration would not be eager to follow the will of Congress. Among these are differing philosophies, partisan political reasons, the resentment of congressional tampering, bureaucratic resistance to change, and reluctance to deal with new concepts. The Executive Branch might have difficulty in trying to carry out the program or for any variety of reasons it might want to stall, delay, or even stifle it; once again then, even with the money in hand, the program's future could be in jeopardy. Congress is able to maintain involvement in the implementation phase through the oversight process.

From a congressional standpoint, following legislation through from conception to a functioning program is a long and continual struggle marked by innumerable crises and decision points, at any one of which the mythical stone could roll back down the hill. The struggle over the Environmental Education Act began in 1969 and was still being waged two years after the bill had been signed into law, when a new danger was approaching—the expiration of the initial period of authorization. At the time of this writing the stone was still being pushed slowly forward.

Interaction: Legislative and Executive

The interaction between the two branches on the Environmental Education Act is related to the fundamental doctrinal issues of checks and balances and separation of powers. Congress was asserting a legislative initiative at a time in which the legislative role was increasingly becoming the province of the Executive Branch. Further, the legislation was not only mandating the Office of Education to establish a program, but directing it how to administer the program in specific terms, a responsibility usually left to the Executive. The Executive Branch quite naturally resisted what it considered an overextension of the congressional role, and thus the separation-of-powers concept was at issue. Through the exercise of its oversight function, Congress brought into play its own powers of checking and balancing to ensure that its will was obeyed. Therefore, the interactions of the two branches of government exhibited the dynamics of both doctrines.

The bill's sponsors, Representative John Brademas and Senator Gaylord Nelson of Wisconsin, felt that in the past years the Executive Branch was threatening to undermine the constitutional prerogatives of Congress in a variety of ways. One of these was to ignore or openly flout the congressional will as expressed in public law.

Congress and the Administration came into conflict over the Environmental Education Act from the time the bill was proposed. The Office of Education first took the position that while it was in sympathy with the purpose of the bill it did not need further legislation to achieve those purposes and announced plans to carry out an environmental education effort. The Administration was firmly opposed in principle to any further grant-in-aid programs; it was attempting to consolidate wherever possible, rather than allowing further proliferation in what was already a maze of programs within HEW and other executive agencies. Once the bill had been passed the Office changed its stance to one of reluctant support. The Administration then opposed a formal appropriation of money to carry out the intent of the legislation and, consequently, did not give the program the priority or the attention the congressional sponsors had intended. The confrontation continued in oversight hearings, which included threats from the Congress concerning the future of other programs the Administration cherished. The Office of Education blamed its slow performance on normal "bureaucratic delay," the time lag necessary to getting results in any huge, multi-layered organization.

Throughout the history of the legislation the atmosphere between the two branches was one of tension. Both branches were favorably disposed toward the concept of environmental education, but due to their own institutional natures they were opposed as to the means by which it could be accomplished. Congress was the initiator in this case, and it proposed a program the Executive Branch felt was unnecessary and therefore could not support with any enthusiasm. As the interaction continued, Congress began not to believe that the Executive Branch would undertake what it said it would. This belief intensified later, when the Executive Branch resisted what it perceived as congressional dictation of matters it felt it could handle better on its own.

Tension between the branches can be a creative and productive aspect of the checks-and-balances system. Ideas are introduced, scrutinized, and transformed into reality through this dynamic interaction. The legislative branch checks the executive by holding it accountable to congressional intent and executive branch policy statements. The executive branch exerts its own check by screening and assessing legislative proposals. Both processes help to ensure sufficient public debate before and after a public policy decision is taken.

The debate over checks and balances in the American system of government is as old as the government itself. In the present era, generally referred to as one of presidential government, the locus of federal power has continued to move from Capitol Hill to 1600 Pennsylvania Avenue. The balance has been increasingly more heavily weighted on the side of the executive, threatening to over-turn the system.

The history of the Environmental Education Act drama-tizes the effectiveness of Congressional followthrough, particularly regarding the oversight process, and indicates an area of increasing congressional activity and power.

An Art and Not a Science

Rules and procedures are the basic framework of the legislative process, but the vital dynamics in the making of a law are provided by the people, events, timing, and circumstances involved. The rules are static; the dynamics are what make legislation an art and not a science.

The outcome of any bill is influenced by a great number of variables. The first of these is the personalities of the people who steer the legislation through the two houses, both members of Congress and their staffs. The legislators' interests, influence, political records, committee assign-ments, and ability to maneuver in the political arena are important, as is their degree and sense of commitment to the legislation. Background factors such as the social and political milieu of the times influence the outcome, as do major events and circumstances related to institutional interests.

The elements of political strategy are compromise, bar-gaining, timing, and trade-offs. These are legitimate pro-cedures in the passing of legislation and not necessary evils of the political system as they often are perceived by critics of the legislative branch. Compromise, for example, is a means of resolving conflicting interests. Along with bargaining, it was used in the "mini-conference" held after the Environmental Education Act had been passed by both houses, in which elements of both bills were woven into a final product. A trade-off was involved in forcing the Executive Branch to create an administrative office, with the implicit danger of provoking continuing hostility to the program and causing it to receive a lower funding level. Timing was involved when the congressional sponsors took advantage of the pressures created by the few days remaining before the elections to whip the bill through. There was a sense of urgency in Congress, with the congressmen wanting to get home for the final campaigning, which resulted in a flurry of legislative activity.

In many cases half a loaf is all that was being sought in the first place, and it is compromise that enables legislators to get the half. With the Environmental Education Act the appropriation strategy was generally to go for a higher amount than was thought attainable and to be prepared to take what the sponsors knew they could realistically expect.

The path each bill follows is governed by a strategy that is generated from the circumstances involved; thus, strategy changes as conditions change. The legislative strategy is flexible, and fall-back positions must be ready in case something should go wrong. At each decision point are several alternative courses of action, and there is usually a great deal of uncertainty about the short- and long-term implications of the possible options. Seat-of-the-pants decisions, rather than prolonged deliberation, are the rule due to the pressures of time. Finally, an indispensable ingredient in any successful legislative formula is luck.

The history of the Environmental Education Act epitomizes the continuing nature of making a legislative idea reality. It involved all three major functions of Congress —legislation, appropriation, and oversight—and it offers insight into the interaction and the necessary tension between the legislative and executive branches and the workings of the checks-and-balances system. Moreover, it demonstrates that Congress is perhaps more able than is often thought to innovate a legislative idea and to follow through with it to implement a national policy.

The Eagle Has Landed: Societal Impulses

HOUSTON: 30 seconds.

EAGLE: Forward. Drifting right. Contact light. Okay, engine stop. ALA out of detent. Modes control both auto, descent engine command override, off. Engine arm, off. 413 is in.

HOUSTON: We copy you down, Eagle.

EAGLE (ARMSTRONG): Houston, Tranquility Base here. The Eagle has landed.

The year the Environmental Education Act was introduced, 1969, was one of dazzling technological triumph for America. A decade of tremendous scientific achievement was climaxed on July 20, when Neil Armstrong and Buzz Aldrin set down their fragile, spiderlike craft called the Eagle in the moon's Sea of Tranquility. For the first time in history man had escaped his own environment to walk on another body in space. The moon landing was a symbol of man's progress in the direction Western civilization was taking him, and at the same time it was a dramatization of the true nature of the world from which he had come.

The Apollo 11 astronauts, like the space voyagers who preceded them, saw the earth from a new vantage point. No longer the vast and limitless universe of man's activities, the earth now appeared as an isolated blue-green ball turning slowly in space. It was closed, self-sustaining, finite. Secondly, it was obvious that their escape from the earth was a momentary illusion. Their dependence upon the home planet was made dramatically evident in the complex apparatus they carried with them to survive outside its atmosphere. Third, the delicate system of the spacecraft was demonstrating something about the earth itself. The concept of "Spaceship Earth"—that the earth, like the spacecraft, is an enclosed life-support system with a limited and exhaustible stock of resources—became a rallying cry for the new environmental movement that emerged at the end of the decade.

The American public began awakening to the environmental crisis in the 1960s, but environmental quality did not become a national political issue until almost ten years later. The first warnings of the possibly disastrous results of man's activities went largely unheard, but in 1962 Rachel Carson opened a floodgate of environmental concern with her powerful indictment of man's irresponsible use of pesticides, in her book *Silent Spring*. Point by point she presented chilling evidence that the chlorinated hydrocarbons of DDT and other pesticides were moving up the life chains to threaten the extinction of entire species of wildlife, to contaminate the rivers and oceans, even the world's underground seas, and to be stored in the fatty tissues of the human body, with gruesome and unknown implications for the future of mankind.

Silent Spring had a tremendous emotional impact on the public consciousness. It was met with shock and incredulity; some damned it as inaccurate and propagandistic. Whatever its real faults, for the first time an environmental issue had created widespread public furor. Further, the book enlightened the public, as well as much of the scientific community, about the interrelatedness of contaminants and all aspects of the environment. The book became a best-seller, and a year later Miss Carson's findings were largely confirmed in a report issued by President Kennedy's Science Advisory Committee.

The public responded, and the environment became the subject of a new mass movement. Citizens groups, such as GASP (Group Against Smog and Pollution) in Pittsburgh, were organized to attack local environmental problems, and the problems themselves became political and economic issues at local levels. Environmental action groups prepared to sue polluters. Youth rallied behind the green-on-white environmental banner and adopted the environment as a cause, as they and their predecessors had done with civil rights and ending the Vietnam War. Rather rapidly, the environment was becoming a national issue.

The most important single event in focusing attention on the environment was the first Earth Day, April 22, 1970. Earth Day was conceived as an occasion for teach-ins, conferences, seminars, and other types of public environmental activities on a nationwide basis. It was the creation of Senator Gaylord Nelson, who proposed the idea and subsequently invited Republican Representative Paul McCloskey of California to co-sponsor it with him. It involved some 10 million people in 2,000 communities, 2,000 colleges and universities, and 10,000 elementary and high schools across the country. Congress was recessed for the day, with many legislators pressed into environmental speaking tours. Its most important effect, as Nelson said a year later, was to ensure, for the first time, that the issue of environmental quality became a part of the national political dialogue, "forcing every public leader in government, schools, churches, business, labor, to take notice." Earth Day both stimulated active citizen participation and demonstrated that environmental quality was a subject of widespread public concern, and it helped establish environmental quality as a political issue that would have to be resolved at the national level.

Earth Day events covered a wide range of activities, from demonstrations, rallies, speeches, classroom sessions of all types, litter pickups, and beautification efforts such as tree and flower planting. According to the press director of Environmental Action, Inc., the group established to coordinate Earth Day, it was "part festival of spring, part deadly serious protest—a bizarre outpouring of Boy Scouts, businessmen, campus militants, middle Americans, and the entire population of Woodstock Nation."

In San Diego, California, and Topeka, Kansas, students went to school on roller skates and skate boards, horses and bicycles to avoid riding in automobiles or buses. In New York, Philadelphia, and other cities, the traffic was banned from specified areas during the day. In Boulder, Colorado, the use of electricity was curtailed to demonstrate a need to reduce the air pollution caused by generating electricity. In Louisville, Kentucky, 1,500 pupils crowded into a school concourse to illustrate the problem of overpopulation. Elementary school children held litter pickups, and the Reynolds Metals Company sponsored projects at 18 colleges to collect and recycle aluminum cans.

Earth Day made good news copy, and the media did all they could to publicize it, even to the extent of making activities seem more significant than they were.

Some were skeptical. A small sampling of Harvard Business School students by the *Christian Science Monitor* indicated that they were unimpressed with Earth Day. They were pessimistic that progress could be made because they didn't trust business, which they said was responsible for the environmental problem, to solve it. They pointed out that the American economic system is geared to higher levels of production and consumption every year, and they felt that the government is not free enough from business influence to enact the bold measures necessary to reverse the environmental deterioration. The Daughters of the American Revolution called the environmental movement "distorted and exaggerated," and a member from Missouri reportedly said during a debate, "This is one of the subversive element's last steps."

On the whole, Earth Day publicized the environmental crisis and stimulated public debate about what could be done to meet it. Shortly afterward, Earth Week was proclaimed as an annual event, to be held during the third week of every April. Environmental law firms came into existence to take the "public interest" as clients in lawsuits against polluters. Old-line conservation organizations such as the National Audubon Society and the National Wildlife Federation lobbied in Washington alongside newer and more activist groups such as the Environmental Foundation, Zero Population Growth, and Friends of the Earth.

Meanwhile Congress and other branches of the federal government were responding to the pressures for enhancing environmental quality.

THE FEDERAL RESPONSE

The federal government had been enacting and implementing legislation to control air and water pollution for two decades, but it was not until the Ninety-first Congress (1969–71) that environmental quality became a high-priority issue. The history of federal pollution control efforts has been involved with the question of states' rights, since before 1948 legal authority in this area belonged almost exclusively to state and local governments. The first important federal legislation to control pollution was the Water Pollution Control Act of 1948. However, the Act was weak and too dependent upon the states, and the provisions for its enforcement by the Public Health Service were considered unworkable. The Act was amended in 1956 to strengthen its enforcement procedures, but the federal government still had to get consent from the states involved before it could initiate federal court action against polluters. This problem was resolved with a 1961 amendment.

As environmental awareness increased in the wake of *Silent Spring*, the federal government began to feel that the states were not doing enough to control pollution. The Water Quality Act, which was introduced in 1963 and enacted in 1965, set forth a national policy of enhancing water quality and established the Federal Water Pollution

Control Administration. It also established a program for setting water quality standards. This legislation was followed by the Clean Water Restoration Act of 1966, which authorized grants for constructing municipal waste-treatment facilities, and by the Water Quality Improvement Act of 1970, which strengthened federal authority to deal with specific problems such as oil pollution, in particular response to pressures created by the Santa Barbara "blowout" of 1969.

Federal air-pollution legislation began in 1955, when Congress authorized a yearly $5 million for the Public Health Service to conduct research on air pollution and possible means of controlling it. In 1963 Congress passed the first major air-pollution legislation, the Clean Air Amendments Act, authorizing HEW to carry out additional research and providing grants for state, regional, and local agencies to create or to improve their own regulatory programs. The federal government was given limited enforcement power. The Motor Vehicle Control Act of 1965 added powers to set emission standards for new automobiles. In 1967 the Air Quality Act enunciated a national policy of air quality along the lines of the 1965 Water Quality Act and provided for designating air-quality control regions and setting air-quality standards. The major responsibility remained with the individual states.

The Clean Air Amendment Act of 1970 greatly expanded the federal role. It authorized for the first time the setting of standards at a national level for pollution from stationary sources, strengthened and accelerated the enforcement of new automobile-emission standards, and provided for the initiation of citizen suits. It also established a Noise Abatement and Control Office.

In the area of solid-waste disposal, legislation in 1965

authorized research, development, and demonstration; in 1970 the Resources Recovery Act, provided financial assistance to the states for the construction of solid-waste disposal facilities and directed HEW to carry out research into waste recovery and recycling.

The trend of the Ninety-first Congress was toward giving the federal government direct authority to deal with pollution. The 1970 Clean Air Amendments Act, for example, not only allowed the federal government to set standards, but also provided the tools whereby the standards could be enforced.

More than 2,000 bills related to environmental quality were introduced in the Ninety-first Congress. Of these, 121 became public law, out of a total of 695 bills signed during both sessions. The thrust of the legislation was to take a point-by-point approach to the environmental issue, dealing with specific aspects of larger problems, such as reducing auto-exhaust emissions as a means of controlling air pollution. The federal response relied upon regulatory means to carry out its goals. Environmental control efforts were often expressed in terms of numbers and quantities that would be applied with regard to each problem.

The goal of achieving and maintaining environmental quality had not yet been stated as a comprehensive national policy, and no grand strategy had evolved for reaching the goal. The situation at the end of the decade has been likened to the early 1930s, when a variety of different programs relating to the most pressing national goal at that time—economic recovery—were established within the federal bureaucracy, and all claimed to be helping improve economic conditions.

The goal was formally defined by the National Environmental Policy Act of 1969, which declared it federal policy:

> To use all practicable means and measures, including
> financial and technical assistance, in a manner cal-
> culated to foster and promote the general welfare, to
> create and maintain conditions under which man and
> nature can exist in productive harmony, and fulfill
> the social, economic, and other requirements of pres-
> ent and future Americans.

The Act also required that prior to taking any action "significantly affecting the quality of the human environment," every federal agency would prepare a detailed
statement presenting the environmental impact of the proposed action. Another provision of the Act was to establish
a Council on Environmental Quality in the Executive
Office of the President, parallel to the President's Council
of Economic Advisors.

The Environmental Education Act of 1970 was an attempt to approach the goal of environmental quality
through citizen enlightenment and activism rather than
through regulatory law and standards enforcement. It proposed a nationwide educational effort to provide for environmental learning as a means of dealing with the
environmental problem on a long-term, continuous basis.

Beginnings of the Environmental Education Act

The passage of federal legislation depends upon a complex
and sometimes fortuitous combination of timing and
events. Equally important are the personalities of the Congressmen and staffs involved. Conditions were right for the
introduction of an environmental education act, but the
act would probably not have come into existence as it did

without the initial and sustained efforts of Indiana Representative John Brademas and Senator Gaylord Nelson of Wisconsin, both Democrats. Because the bill was successful in completing the legislative process, these two, in retrospect, can be said to have been exactly the right people for this bill.

Brademas and Nelson, along with their staffs, played very different roles in the bill's history, and both were indispensable at certain points in its progress. Essentially, Brademas wrote the legislation and brought it into the political forum; Nelson backed it in the Senate and ensured that it would not die from lack of funding. Others were influential in the bill's passage, and among these were other members of Congress, staff members and a few mavericks in the bureaucracy.

John Brademas was an ideal man to introduce the Environmental Education Act. A former Rhodes scholar, Brademas had established a reputation as a combination of the scholar and the practical, successful legislator. He had been in Congress since 1958, and as a consequence of his assignment on the Education and Labor Committee, had created a strong legislative record and constituency in the areas of elementary and secondary education, higher education, and vocational education. He was involved in juvenile-delinquency control, the Teacher Corps, and teacher fellowships. He authored the International Education Act, sponsored the National Commission on Libraries and Information Sciences Act, and co-sponsored the Drug Abuse Education Act.

Brademas was proud of his academic connections, and he valued his reputation in the academic and legislative communities. He was not the kind of man to introduce a bill in his area of expertise for publicity purposes alone, and he would not have staked his reputation on an idea unless he thought it had at least a fair chance to become law.

Brademas felt very strongly that Congress can and should play a significant role as initiator and creator of public policy. As a professional politician he was committed to his legislative task of seeing ideas he felt were important become translated into reality. He was willing to commit himself to a legislative idea, as he did with the Environmental Education Act, and to pursue it, as he found he had to, well into its implementation phase. Further, the Environmental Education Act was his baby; he authored it, he felt responsible for it, and as its difficulties continued he would be prepared to take on the Executive Branch tenaciously to save it.

As Chairman of the House Select Subcommittee on Education Brademas was in a good position to introduce the bill, have it referred to his subcommittee, and get it to the floor of the House. The resources of the subcommittee staff were at his disposal, and his political position regarding education legislation gave him a degree of power in dealing with the federal education establishment.

Finally, the environmental response was becoming a burning and timely political issue in late 1969, and it clearly would remain so for the future. This bill gave Brademas a perfect opportunity to move into the environmental area, and such opportunities would be limited for members of the Education Committee.

For Nelson, too, the issue was ideal. He was a life-long conservationist whose political career had sprung from the Progressive heritage of Wisconsin. Since entering the Senate in 1962 he had established himself as an early and constant advocate of enhancing environmental quality and as an independent liberal who very carefully reserved his right to dissent. Nelson was also a practical politician.

His independence and practicality had been developed during his early experience as a minority-party member of the State Senate and then as Governor of Wisconsin. During his two terms as Governor Nelson accomplished the creation of a landmark program to develop and protect state recreation resources, along with a sweeping tax-reform measure, despite the fact that he was facing an unfriendly legislature. In these circumstances he had to have a realistic view of the forces involved in the legislative process and achieve his goals through persuasion and skillful maneuvering.

In the U.S. Senate Nelson had taken a lonely stand as one of the first dissenters against further U.S. involvement in Vietnam and had prepared an amendment to the 1964 Tonkin Gulf Resolution (not introduced at the urging of Senator William Fulbright, Chairman of the Foreign Relations Committee) to preclude the use of U.S. ground-combat forces. He was one of the early opponents of the Anti-Ballistic-Missile System, and he crusaded against the use of herbicides in Vietnam. In other areas Nelson had achieved legislative measures in the fields of tire and auto safety and had co-authored the Teacher Corps Act. He was familiar with federal-education measures and program implementation.

Nelson had staked out his claim in the environmental area and had a record of legislative efforts to preserve wilderness and wildlife and to regulate pesticide use and solid-waste disposal, among other subjects. He had contacts and credentials along with respect from his Senate colleagues in this field. Brademas' introduction of the Environmental Education Act happened to coincide with

Nelson's own efforts and deeply felt convictions about Earth Day and about the need for increasing nationwide public awareness of the environmental issue.

Nelson was less involved with the politics of education than was Brademas, and he did not chair an education subcommittee. However, he was a member of the Senate Labor and Public Welfare Committee, which is the parent committee for education, and was thus in a good position to initiate legislation.

The differing records of Nelson and Brademas reflect the difference in committee assignments between the two houses and, to some extent, the different roles of the representative and the senator. Representatives are members of one major committee and frequently receive one or more secondary committee assignments, while senators are assigned to at least three committees. When the Environmental Education Act was being passed, Brademas was a member of the minor House Administration Committee, besides Education and Labor, and Nelson was on four committees: Labor and Public Welfare, Interior and Insular Affairs, Select Nutrition and Human Needs, and the Select Small Business Committee.

With wider-ranging committee assignments, a senator has a broader scope of activity than a representative. Consequently, he must spread his interests over a greater number of areas. He is compensated for this seeming disadvantage by having a much larger staff, which can assist in focusing his attention in a single field. The senator also benefits from the cross-pollinization of ideas resulting from the smaller size of the Senate and its more flexible rules of procedure, which allow for significant activity and debate on the chamber floor. The combination of size and informality within the co-called "club" leads to more frequent and productive personal contacts between the members, allowing a senator to get a good amount of his legislative business accomplished on the floor. In the House the committee system is dominant, allowing far less chance for significant change when bills come to the floor for action.

Behind the scenes most of the day-to-day tasks of legislation in both houses are carried out by staff aides, who may be employed in the congressman's office or on one of his subcommittee staffs. If staffers work for a subcommittee, they will act as legislative experts in the subcommittee's particular area of interest. If they are employed in the congressman's office, their range of responsibilities will be more general, but they will still have the responsibility for various subject areas. Professional staffers can act as advisors, speechwriters, practical politicians, advocates, and research assistants.

There tends to be a difference between the two houses in the role played by the staff members. On both sides an aide can be at one extreme an idea man and on the other a "runner," or "legman." He can be an initiator, injecting something of his own style and priorities into the legislative process, or he can be a passive reactor. The role of a representative's aide always falls somewhere between the two extremes, but a Senate aide generally has more freedom of movement and more power than his House counterpart. The Senate role involves advocacy, initiative, and persistence, and aides often vie with each other for the senator's time. The staffer usually must sell the senator on an idea, focus his attention on it, and make sure he acts at important junctures. The senator must rely heavily on his aides; conversely, they receive a great amount of freedom and trust to work in his behalf. Because of the narrower range of a representative's legislative activities and the much smaller size of his staff, a House aide tends to have a closer and more personal relationship with his employer. He is usually more closely supervised and directed than a Senate aide and has less freedom of initiative. However, all of these characteristics depend to a large extent on the operating style and personality of the congressman, and frequently the opposite is true.

The Brademas and Nelson staffs exemplified these differences. On Brademas' side the staff function was carried out by the employees of the Congressman's Select Education Subcommittee. They received frequent and explicit guidance in the drafting of the bill and its later handling from Brademas, who became deeply and personally involved in the issue. However, they had latitude to maneuver and to contribute significantly to shaping the legislation.

On Nelson's side an aide presented the legislative idea to the Senator, convinced him to introduce and support the Brademas bill, and kept his attention focused on the issue as it progressed. While the bill was compatible with Nelson's personal philosophy, particularly his feelings about Earth Day and the need for an increase in public awareness of the environmental issue, he, as a senator, was never as deeply involved as Brademas. His aide's task was to see that he did not miss an opportunity to help nudge it along or to save it at crucial points.

Introduction of the Bill

The Environmental Education Act was introduced in mid-November 1969 by Congressman Brademas. It was a congressional initiative, but its sources were multiple.

The Act was generated in the grass-roots response to the environmental crisis, which was suddenly becoming a national political issue. Brademas was keenly aware of the environmental problem. He considered it one of the key issues that would have to be addressed through nation-wide educational programs, and he decided to propose legislation to accomplish this. At the same time a few civil servants with the Office of Education were attempting to generate enthusiasm for an environmental education program in their own agency, and had begun proselytizing on Capitol Hill for legislation that would accomplish this. One of the staffs they contacted was that of Brademas' Select Subcommittee on Education. Following a highly emotional presentation by one of the Office of Education employees, the Subcommittee counsel was convinced that the idea was a good one, and he enthusiastically supported the Congressman's decision to draft and introduce the bill.

It is a fairly common pattern of initiation for a lower-level employee of a government agency to quietly put a bug in the ear of congressional staff aides about legislative ideas that affect the employee's own agency but that are not being officially sought by the incumbent administration. This is also an effective means of informal interaction between the two branches of government. Sometimes the idea for new legislation seems to appear in so many places at the same time that the actual source is impossible to identify. In this case the idea moved vertically in both branches—from staff to bosses and bosses to staff—and back and forth horizontally from staff in one branch to staff in the other.

Brademas directed his subcommittee staff to begin working on an environmental education bill, patterned after the Drug Abuse Education Act, which he had sponsored. The subcommittee had recently drafted the drug abuse bill, which was then before the Senate after having just passed the House. The staff began preparing the environmental education bill in the fall of 1969. They borrowed the general format of the drug abuse education bill and, where appropriate, lifted whole paragraphs verbatim and inserted "the environment" and "ecology" for "drug abuse." The major difference, at this point in the bill's history, was to add the provision that an advisory council be established to guide and assist the program. The idea was not to write a definitive bill but, in keeping with Brademas' philosophy, to create a broad and open-ended legislative proposal that could be refined during the hearing process.

Another consideration was to shape the bill so that it would be referred to Brademas' subcommittee. The jurisdiction of each of the House education subcommittees is specified in the full committee rules, adopted at the beginning of every congressional term. Under the committee rules a bill initiated by a committee member would be referred to the appropriate subcommittee by the committee chairman, regardless of whether or not the author is a member of the subcommittee.

The Select Subcommittee was responsible for special-education programs, and the staff had to choose its words carefully to ensure that the bill would provide for a "special" program. If too much emphasis was placed on elementary, secondary and vocational education, it might go to the General Subcommittee on Education, which had jurisdiction in this area, but the major concern was that it be kept out of the Special Subcommittee on Education of Representative Edith Green (D–Ore.), which had authority over "education beyond the high school level." Her subcommittee had the reputation of being voracious in its appetite for new legislation.

During the writing phase the staff members were in close contact with the Office of Education employees who had helped initiate the idea and with the Legislative Reference Service in the Library of Congress (now the Congressional Reference Service). With the drafting completed, Brademas introduced the bill in the House on November 12, and it was referred back to his subcommittee for action.

On the Senate side this exact bill was introduced one week later by Senator Gaylord Nelson, and the bill was referred to the Subcommittee on Education of the Committee on Labor and Public Welfare. Nelson's staff had been involved with the idea for some time, and had been well informed of Brademas' progress. Nelson's decision to introduce that particular bill at that time was influenced in large part by a subtle but important factor.

Senate interest in environmental education was not restricted to Nelson's office. Senator Charles E. Goodell (R–N.Y.) had already asked his staff to prepare legislation on this subject. Goodell, who had filled the seat vacated after the assassination of Robert Kennedy, was coming up for his first senatorial election in 1970. To many members of the Senate who had had more time to establish a reputation, he was a "Charlie-come-lately" who was getting into every legislative initiative within reach in order to make a name for himself as fast as possible. He was running a hard race. Even the Nixon Administration was out to unseat him by supporting Conservative Party candidate James Buckley.

The prominence of the environmental issue gave him

and his staff incentive to move into an area long dominated by many others. Nelson was not about to let Goodell preempt this opportunity, and he introduced Brademas' Environmental Education Act in the Senate almost a month before Goodell was able to present his own Environmental Reclamation Education Act on December 11, 1969.

In addition to Nelson's wanting to claim the credit as chief sponsor (a human desire that does not escape members of Congress any more than it does those in other institutions) there was a sound political reason for beating Goodell to the punch. The New Yorker was not a member of the Senate Labor and Public Welfare Committee, which had jurisdiction over the measure. His bill would not receive the attention of a bill authored by a member of the committee, and the education subcommittee with its Democratic chairman would not be eager to give priority to a bill with a Republican stamp on it for a Republican who was up for reelection.

If Goodell had introduced an environmental education bill first, the initiative would have been credited to him regardless of what form Nelson might have chosen for a separate bill. Therefore, in order to advance the political cause of environmental education, the best approach seemed to be to bypass Goodell rather than letting him take the lead or to join forces with him.

A basic question raised at this stage concerns the degree of commitment that Brademas, Nelson, and their staffs were willing to give for enactment of the measure. Was it: (1) window dressing, i.e., introduced for immediate publicity reasons; (2) a wait-and-see measure with enough potential to warrant a moderate initial input of time and effort; or (3) an idea "whose time had come," justifying all the backing that could be given it to get it passed?

The sponsors of the Environmental Education Act did not view it as one of the thousands of bills destined to go nowhere for lack of timeliness, interest, and support; nor did they consider it red-hot. For the time being the bill fitted into category two. The increasing public outcry on environmental deterioration and the outpouring of support for upcoming Earth Day made it apparent that the move was timely. As the bill advanced through the legislative process, it was transformed from the status of a measure with high potential to the category of an idea whose time had come.

As with any proposal a member of Congress believes has a reasonable chance of getting passed, the formal commitment to the bill on the part of Brademas and Nelson was unequivocal from the beginning. Because of this, environmental education was guaranteed at least its day in court. The strategy then would be an activist approach that would result, at the very minimum, in hearings to be held in early 1970.

Strategy Formulation

The formulation of a long-range legislative strategy is imposible except within the most general guidelines. The procedural constraints are a given factor, and the goal is known. But the path to the goal is dependent upon constantly changing realities. The constraints of realpolitik are not in the rules and cannot be formalized. A legislative strategy must always be flexible to deal with the unpredictable milieu through which the bill will pass.

When the bill was introduced, many factors were expected to figure into the decision-making process. These were the "givens" upon which the general strategy for passage was formulated. In their simplest form they amount to the tensions within the legislative and executive branches and between them over questions of the separation of powers, checks and balances, partisanship, and the nature of the bureaucracy.

The odds against any bill being enacted into law by Congress are formidable, especially for a legislative proposal embracing a new idea. During the previous Ninetieth Congress (1967 and 1968), a staggering total of almost 30,000 legislative measures were introduced in both houses. Some were simple joint and concurrent resolutions, but the great majority (about 25,000) were bills. Of these 25,000 only 640 actually became law. The number of successes comes out to one-quarter of one percent. Many of these were extensions of existing programs, which authorized continued funding; some extended deadlines or jurisdictions; and some proclaimed this day or that week, such as "Howdy Doody Day."

It was almost certain that the bill would meet opposition from the Administration for three reasons. First, the Environmental Education Act was a congressional initiative, and any administration is zealous in guarding what it perceives as its own prerogatives. The Nixon Administration, in particular, enjoyed less than cordial relations with the legislative branch. It repeatedly expressed its strong distaste and contempt for congressional interference in policy formulation. Ideas that were injected into debates by Congressional leaders, in the form of legislation or otherwise, were often given lip service or ignored. The legislative branch would have more than normal difficulty in making the Environmental Education Act law because of this pervasive hostility.

Second, the bill would establish a new subject matter or "categorical" program, and Administration philosophy was firmly opposed to the proliferation of programs and categories, as will be discussed later. It explicitly attempted to consolidate and bring programs together whenever possible for efficiency, control, and ease of management. This was the Administration's major objection, and it held to the position that it had enough authority under legislation already in existence to carry out the goals of the Environmental Education Act.

Third, the combination of a Republican Administration and a Democratic Congress created an additional friction because the primary sponsors were both Democrats. Brademas made a special point of getting bipartisan co-sponsorship from the beginning in order to prevent the Administration from considering the House bill a Democratic measure.

Nelson did not request co-sponsorship before he introduced the bill in the Senate, and when he solicited for co-sponsors shortly thereafter, only one of the twenty-four affirmative responses was from a Republican, the late Winston L. Prouty (R–Vt.). The main reason for this imbalance in the Senate was that the Goodell bill was due to emerge soon, and many Republican senators knew about it. When it was introduced less than a month later, the co-sponsors were seven Republicans and one Democrat. Prouty would probably have supported the Goodell measure had he known about it in advance.

Working relations between the two branches of government are compounded when partisan issues, real or perceived, arise. The Administration would not want to give credit to a Democratic initiative in the Congress, and to a lesser extent the Democratic leadership would not want to support a Goodell bill over a Nelson bill. The bill was always bipartisan in the House, and it received strong bipartisan support as it progressed through the Senate. However, it was considered a partisan matter by the Nixon Administration.

Perhaps collaboration between Nelson and Goodell at the outset might have been a wiser course to follow. The partisan tone would have been muted in the Senate at the expense of sharing the leadership with someone who was nearly unknown for activities in educational reform and improving environmental quality and who had few friends in the Executive Branch.

The initial strategy was simply to apply persistent enough pressure to overcome the terrific odds against passage. The small group of Congressmen and their staffs had to exert maximum influence at the right times, or the inertia and resistance of both the Executive Branch and Congress itself would be too hard to overcome. This meant moving the bill through quickly, particularly because the upcoming elections would cause a long pause in the legislative process. Both congressional sponsors determined that there could be no more appropriate means of giving the bill the necessary momentum than through holding dramatic and dynamic hearings.

3

Hearings

PURPOSE OF HEARINGS

WITHOUT A SET of hearings, a bill's chances for passage are virtually nil. Hearings publicize the issue, help to develop a constituency for it, assist in legitimizing the bill's purpose, and help to refine and sharpen its content. The record of the hearings becomes a source document providing a cogent argument in favor of the bill's passage and indicating how well its case has been made and the degree to which the sponsors are committed to it.

Soon after the Environmental Education Act was introduced, the Nelson and Brademas staffs began preparing to hold hearings on the bill by soliciting ideas and information to accomplish these purposes. The hearings that were subsequently scheduled lasted for thirteen days in the House and for two days in the Senate. Four of the fifteen days were spent in New York, San Francisco, and Los Angeles.

The resulting hearing documents totaled 1,307 pages of testimony, letters, and supporting statements. More than 90 witnesses testified, and among these were students, a theologian, educators, philosophers, an artist, environmentalists, businessmen, and government officials. Their testimony represented a broad range of knowledgeable viewpoints on environmental education and closely related areas and included lively sessions of dialogue between witnesses and subcommittee members that helped to sharpen the bill and contributed to the overall argument for it.

The hearings served to move the level of debate on environmental education from intellectual circles into the national arena. Environmental education became a political concern of the federal government, and the debate centered around questions of governmental policies, priorities, and programs.

The need was for changing public values to cope with the newly perceived environmental crisis. The proposed solution was legislation to create an environmental education program. It was necessary to see if environmental education as described and defined in the hearings could be a major step in that direction.

It was especially important for the sponsors of this bill to hear suggestions for additions and improvements. The legislators were pushing into a new field of public policy in which there were no political experts. The task of the sponsors was to develop environmental education as a matter of national policy and translate that policy into a specific program. The hearings were designed to serve that purpose. The legislators would use the hearings to add substance and insight to their arguments, increasing their own expertise in the task of moving the bill through the legislative process. They would also be given access to the widest possible range of ideas relating to environmental education.

THE HEARINGS: HOUSE

The task of the Brademas and Nelson staffs during preparation for the hearings was to select witnesses who could provide the most incisive testimony on the merits and deficiencies of the bill. Successful hearings are indicated by the caliber of witnesses, the effectiveness of the testimony, the excitement of the debate, and the number of specific recommendations that become part of the bill.

Brademas and his staff began planning the hearings in December 1969, about a month ahead of their Senate counterparts. Maureen Orth, an independent consultant from San Francisco, was hired specifically to work on the hearings with the two Subcommittee staff members, Jack Duncan and Ronald Katz.

They began sorting through names of people to identify potential witnesses for the hearings. The next step was to write nearly a hundred people and solicit their views on the proposal. These responses and numerous telephone conversations provided the principal basis for selecting witnesses and a source of suggestions for the later rewriting of the bill.

The hearings began in late March, bracketing Earth Day (April 22), and ended on May 2, 1970. Nine of the thirteen days of hearings were held in the capital, with two days in New York and one day each in San Francisco and Los Angeles. The hearings opened with an overview of the broader aspects of the environmental issue by an ecologist, theologian, and an artist. On the second day college and high school students were invited to comment on the bill, a practice not common for congressional hearings. Most of the remaining witnesses in Washington were Establishment types used to speaking on Capitol Hill and familiar with the environmental education issues. In New York and California the story was different. An attempt was made to reach to the grass-roots level of concern over the environmental issue. The witnesses were mainly people associated in one way or another with the environmental problem at a local level. These days of hearings gave color and depth to the hearings by providing earthiness, candor, and an exposure to local rather than national perspectives.

The peppery Miss Orth suggested to Brademas a day of psychedelic hearings—with strobe lights, slide projectors, flashing and moving lights on the walls, and rock music during the testimony—but this was too much even for Brademas. Overall, the hearings were exciting and had a flair of the age of Spaceship Earth.

THE HEARINGS: SENATE

The extensive House hearings left little additional ground to be covered by the Senate Subcommittee on Education. There was no need on the Senate side to duplicate the lengthy House record. The best approach was to choose witnesses whose testimony would complement that presented in the House. The only exception to not asking previous witnesses to testify again was inviting the Commissioner of Education to appear; it is usual for the top official of an executive agency to testify on proposed legislation effecting his agency.

On February 13, 1970, Senator Nelson addressed a letter to a number of people requesting their views on several questions related to the Environmental Education Act. Again, as with the approach used in the House, those queried represented a broad spectrum of backgrounds and experiences. The responses became a helpful part of the hearing record and also provided a basis for selecting witnesses for the two days of hearings.

The hearings were held on May 19 and 20 and brought out some additional ideas about programs and broadened the notion of what environmental education was. The marine element of environmental education was added to the overall hearing record. The idea was emphasized that the ocean, coastal, and wetland areas, all are just as important teaching resources as the land environment but are often inadvertently overlooked.

In spite of the fact that Senator Nelson was not a member of the Senate Subcommittee on Education, the Subcommitte Chairman, Claiborne Pell (D–R.I.), took a rare step in the Senate and indicated that he was willing to allow Nelson to serve as temporary chairman of his subcommittee for the hearings on the bill, as long as Nelson's staff did the lion's share of the work in setting them up. This was done out of Nelson's own office by one of his legislative assistants, Dennis W. Brezina.

The staffs of Senator Nelson and of the Brademas and Pell subcommittees worked together closely during this period. They exchanged information and ideas and explored key questions on both sides of the Hill to elevate the quality of the hearings. The hearings, in turn, increased the excitement of the staffers involved. There was mounting pressure for moving the bill to the floors of the House and Senate. The hearings had set the stage for what was to come, and enthusiasm was on the rise. Enactment seemed more than just a dim possibility.

What Kind of Race of Men?—The Need for Change

On the first day of hearings before the House subcommittee the issue of environmental education was placed in a broad philosophical and spiritual context. The unusual opening testimony set a highly intellectual tone for the discussions on specific topics that would follow.

An ecology professor, LaMont Cole, talked about the meaning of ecology and the need for an ecological, or holistic, approach to problems such as population control. Theologian Joseph Sittler said that the Judeo-Christian tradition commonly understood as man's having dominion over the earth—"that man is given a holy charter to walk through the creation in arrogant haughtiness and do what he pleases with it"—has been misunderstood. In the proper translation of "dominion," which is "to exercise tender care for," he said, "man was ordered so as to live with God's other creation, the earth, that he was to regard her as the object of his guardianship."

The artist Robert Motherwell dealt with the underlying question of values. He eloquently expressed his outrage at modern society's "petrification of human feeling" in pursuit of "the 'real' business of the day." He asked:

> What kind of race of men is it who can rape or vomit
> on the landscape, like drunken soldiers in a conquered

village, or like destructive and greedy little boys let
loose in an enormous toy-and-candy store, to break
and gorge as they like; while other little boys, in other
parts of this planet that we Americans are turning into
a garbage dump, stand with a piece of string and an
orange as their treasures?

He said he did not know how to legislate "the growth of
human awareness," or how to "make shameful insensitivity
to landscape," but if the present bill could do either or
both, "who could not favor it?"

The Students

The second day of the House hearings was devoted to
students and young activists in the environmental movement. Their position in the schedule indicated the degree
of priority their testimony was being given. This was a
special characteristic of the hearings. Not only were students contributing, but their testimony would be weighed
carefully, and several of their suggestions would be included in the final legislation.

The hearings lacked real controversy, but they displayed
a great deal of skepticism about the bill's approach and
about the possibility of its provisions being implemented
so that they would work. Some of the greatest skeptics, as
well as some of the most enthusiastic and imaginative supporters of the legislation, were among the students.

Student participation was very important to the bill's
sponsors. The students would have direct and fresh insights into what education was accomplishing or failing to
accomplish, and their viewpoint would be different from

that of the professional educators. Also, the bill had distinctly anti-Establishment reform characteristics that shared something of the counterculture's rebellious spirit. Primarily, the legislators wanted to hear the students' opinions about the proposal and to benefit from their advice.

High school and college students told about programs they were involved in. Following them, Garret De Bell, Washington representative of Zero Population Growth and editor of *The Environmental Handbook*, testified. De Bell had several proposals about getting the money that would be made available under the legislation into the hands of people who would do something with it. He said the grants should not be distributed through university departments:

> After seeing how well the faculty at our universities have enforced specialization at the cost of breadth and have resisted interdisciplinary teaching and research, I would not like to see legislation which lets the fox guard the chicken coop. . . . We have to take the people on the campus that are sympathetic to the basic purpose of the bill and let them get money independently. . . .

Brademas answered that while he lauded De Bell's point of view, it was the framers' hope "that we can help harness some of the existing structure to enable [the bill] to make a greater impact on public awareness." (The thrust of De Bell's ideas, however, was incorporated into the "small grants" section of the bill.)

Denis Hayes, the Director of Environmental Action and the national coordinator for Earth Day, warned against perpetuating in new legislation what he saw as great errors of the American educational system. He said:

> Education is considered to be units of material, delivered by mediocre teachers, measured in credit hours, and marked at discrete intervals by diplomas and graduation to a new stage. This may have been a valid way to train monks in the time of Thomas Aquinas, but today it serves to crush the very creativity we so desperately need. To the extent that this bill encourages that view of education, to the extent that it strengthens institutions which operate on that set of assumptions, it is contributing more to our problems than to their solution.

Like De Bell, he wanted a bill that would force revolutionary change.

Brademas later commented that while he sympathized with much of Hayes' criticism, he would hope that:

> This modest vessel that we have set afloat into the sea will not be expected to bear the whole burden of reforming and revolutionizing the American educational system. . . . That might be hopeful if we could do it, but I don't want to weight it down too heavily.

Stewart Brand, editor of the *Whole Earth Catalog*, went one step further during the later San Francisco hearings. Brand said he was delighted by the spirit behind the bill but "depressed by every measure in it." He felt that voluntary mass education would be poisoned by federal aid. He said "the whole apparatus of application, approval and

funding commonly introduces a dishonesty into an operation that can never be eradicated." He said ecology cannot be taught, but nevertheless it is being learned. "If you
try to teach it to people, you will only teach them to hate
it." He ended with the Beatles' admonition, "Let it be."

Structures That Last

The following days of hearings before both the House and
Senate subcommittees were exploratory and educational for
the bill's sponsors. Basically, they consisted of an attempt
to define what was being done or could be done in the
broad area of environmental education, to indicate ways in
which the proposed legislation could be strengthened.

One of the most farsighted and inventive presentations
was that of the anthropologist Margaret Mead. Her pres-
ence alone was an addition to the hearings and was evidence of the high caliber of the witnesses who agreed to
testify for the bill. She depicted the need for an environmental education program, discussed the problems it
would help deal with, and gave imaginative examples of
what it could accomplish.

She said we would have to learn, and the bill would help
in this, what a "long-term, continuous, and ultimately
rather boring activity" caring for the environment will be.
"It is going to be very much like good housekeeping, you
know, and the dishes are never done."

If the effort were to last, we would have to keep at it:

> The people of the United States are particularly bad
> about maintenance. We have a great tendency to spot

a danger, get very much excited, pass a bill, and then take our marbles and go home. A short-term perspective won't protect the environment. We will have every polluter back polluting cheerfully in five years unless we build structures that will last.

She defined the best kind of structure as:

The continuous participation of children and high school students and college students, but particularly school children in every community, because you have a new crop of them every year, and what we need to look at now is providing regenerative cycles for dealing with problems that are going to be continuous.

She was not for scrapping the existing school system, but for using it as a vehicle for the environmental response in education:

Our school system is very archaic, but it is all we have got. It is also the only way in which young people's insights can be put back into a continual institutional framework.

Granted that the average six-year-old child has a different perception of the world from the average forty-year-old school teacher, and the six-year-old child feels things, having been born here in the space age, that the teacher had to learn as an adult "immigrant" into the last half of the twentieth century and may not have learned in the same way. But unless you can pour this back continually into an educational system, it is impossible to build it into the life of the country.

She suggested setting up environmental models in environmental centers and museums to demonstrate the effects of altering factors in the ecological equation. Computers and complex models could be used to confront all the problems of the environment simultaneously. She said that we should start working on a "whole earth model" and proposed that ecological centers be established with internships on islands:

> At present, I don't know any better way of really educating someone to understand an environment than to give him a small island with a real problem to solve on it, and most of the islands of the world are in terrible trouble, so they could use a large number of interns working on their problems of conservation, of balance, of new crops, of protection of the soil, immigration, of population, and so forth.

She said one of the possibilities of the program envisaged in the bill would be the encouragement of such schools, where "a new kind of practitioner in the task of preserving the world is trained."

An Art of the Possible

A number of educators and others involved professionally in the education field stressed the bill's reform characteristics. They indicated what they felt was wrong with the present system and what could be done to change it, using environmental education as a vehicle.

Dr. David Hawkins, a philosophy professor at the University of Colorado, said his college teaching experience had made him "acutely and sometimes frustratingly aware of the fact that education, like politics, is an art of the possible." He said:

> What this means to a teacher is that the young human mind is not an open filing system in which we teach- ers can store the fruits of society's wisdom, but a highly reactive and selective affair which accepts, re- organizes or rejects what we offer in accordance with its own inner program of readiness, need, and motiva- tion.

He called reading, as it is practiced in most elementary schools, "a mechanical instruction in unmotivated decod- ing," and said that in pursuing a curriculum that minimizes children's contact with the world around them, we make their education dependent upon "an abstract symbolic medium" drained of "vitality and meaning."
He said:

> Progress lies in the evolution of a style of school and classroom organization which engages children far more and far more actively than at present with the natural and human world around them . . .

Hawkins and others were sharpening the definition of environmental education for the legislators. They saw it as a process of teaching and learning related to the British open classroom and presented arguments for using it to revolutionize the educational process.

The Communiversity

Some of the witnesses described environmental programs that were already in operation. They were indicating from a practical standpoint what was being accomplished in the area covered by the legislation and demonstrating that its concept was backed by substance. They defined the parameters of the bill in practical, rather than theoretical terms, familiarizing the legislators with the current state of the art.

One of the presentations described a new environmental/ecological approach to higher education. Chancellor Edward Weidner discussed the "communiversity" of the University of Wisconsin, Green Bay, then in its first year of operation, in which learning is structured around interrelated environmental, rather than disciplinary concepts.

The university was described as being organized into four "theme colleges": Environmental Science, Community Sciences, Human Biology, and Creative Communication. A student's curriculum was structured around a particular problem of the biophysical or social environment. He would choose courses in the various disciplines that would contribute to his understanding of the problem.

In this problem-solving process "chemistry, art, secondary school teaching, and psychology all of a sudden come alive," Weidner said in a speech he submitted for the record. "They are means to a social end. They relate to one another, as well as to the environmental problem."

The documents he submitted said the name "communiversity" came from an attempt to relate the university to its surrounding community. Advisory committees representing local business and industry, professional organizations, government, and voluntary agencies visit the campus on a regular basis.

The objective of the school, Weidner said, was "not to train narrow specialists but to extend a broad, general education on environmental quality to all students regardless of their fields of specialization or their professions."

They Have Never Seen a River

Some of the most important pioneering in environmental education had been done by the Ford Foundation, and a foundation project officer, Edward Ames, discussed programs in which the organization was then involved. These included the Tilton School in Tilton, New Hampshire, with its comprehensive program on water pollution, and the John Dewey High School in New York, which was conducting a program in the marine sciences.

He said a fundamental problem in the educational system is the separation of the very special school environment from that of the community:

> I have gone into classrooms in New York and talked
> to the children and found that they have never seen
> a river although their community may be surrounded
> by rivers on three sides.

He suggested to the subcommittee that a higher priority be placed on fundamental changes involving the relationship between the classroom and the surrounding neighborhood than on "the more conventional work at nature centers and sanctuaries."

Ames' testimony emphasized that the environment is more than the out-of-doors; it is also the urban setting with its ugliness and social problems. "Virtually all learning,"

Ames said, "is coming to grips with one's environment in one way or another."

The Oceans and the County Agent

In some of the testimony new ideas were presented that broadened the definition of environmental education. Professor William Wick, who headed the Oregon State Marine Advisory Program, told the Senate subcommittee about a marine-environmental program in Oregon that was administered through the state's Cooperative Extension Service.

He also described a program called "Seashore Eyes," in which the goal was to increase children's perception by having them explore the intertidal zone on the Oregon coast. "Few people who visit the out-of-doors really see anything," he commented. "We are just not used to looking."

Discussing the program, he said:

> The most important technique of the trip was tipping the class over—getting their heads down and their tails up. After a minute in this position even the most squeamish girls, who could not think about picking up a worm, became involved in the microworld in front of them and nothing else really mattered.

Wick headed the marine side of the Cooperative Extension Service for the state of Oregon. Established under the National Sea Grant College and Program Act, this was the equivalent of the county-agent agricultural advisory program for matters related to the land.

Senator Nelson had mentioned during the preceding testimony that the agricultural extension agent and the

home agent had been in the business of conducting education as an actual environmental situation all along. Nelson
said:

> The classroom was the farmer's own farm and the
> teaching involved all the various methods of land use,
> contour cultivation and planting, and methods of
> breeding and developing stock and the production of
> milk.

Wick suggested that:

> A modest program utilizing environmental quality
> extension specialists, or agents . . . to work with
> schools and the public on environmental understand-
> ing, resources, public policy, and other pertinent sub-
> jects would pay substantial dividends with very little
> cost.

He called the county agent "a specialist in one or several
things" and "a darned good generalist in many things." He
said the agent "knows the political make-up of the county
. . . and how to get things done." His most valuable role,
Wick said, would be as "an excellent arranger." In later
testimony the fact arose that the British educational system included such agents working with the community and
the schools.

Into the Political Forum: The Administration

The hearings gave the bill's sponsors a chance to bring
their legislative proposal into the national political forum

for an initial confrontation with the Executive Branch. Since it was envisioned that the Office of Education would have responsibility for the new program that would be created by successful passage of the bill, the Commissioner of Education, James E. Allen, Jr., was invited to testify.

Although the tone of the Commissioner's testimony remained basically unchanged before both House and Senate subcommittees, the Administration's position shifted 180 degrees between the two sets of hearings, for reasons that will be discussed in Chapter 4. Commissioner Allen said all along that the Administration was entirely in accord with the aims of the bill, but on the House side he said the Administration did not favor its passage because the Office of Education had adequate means at its disposal, under existing legislation, to carry out the purposes of the act. In the Senate hearings six weeks later he announced a reversal of this position.

Before the House subcommittee on April 21 Dr. Allen said he would ask for money in the next fiscal year's budget for environmental education activities, but that "I am advised by my staff, Mr. Chairman, that we do not need additional authority to carry out the purposes of H.R. 14753." He assured the legislators that the problem was one of budgetary constraints and not of legislative authority. By this time Allen had established his own personal commitment to environmental education in public speeches and in his efforts to increase environmental-education activities in the Office of Education, as will be discussed later.

Brademas was not pleased with the Administration's stance. He replied to the Commissioner:

It is a cause of great distress to me to see once again in the field of much needed education legislation, it appears all we are getting from the administration is rhetoric, high-sounding prose, but no action and no flesh at all on the bones of the contention that "we mean business." They mean business for the Bureau of the Budget, but no business for the urgent need of education.

At the Senate hearings, due to intervening political events within the Administration, the Commissioner announced on behalf of the Administration that "we welcome very strongly the bipartisan support which Congress has given the bill and we therefore support this legislation."

The Commissioner did suggest a few amendments to the bill, however, principally that the authority in the bill be placed directly under the Secretary of Health, Education and Welfare, and not under the Commissioner of Education, as intended by the lawmakers. The reason, Allen said, is that more agencies than the Office of Education are involved, and the proposal would make it clear that the program "is an entire HEW obligation."

The first round of confrontation between the executive and legislative branches on the Environmental Education Act, then, ended with a token pledge of Administration support for the bill.

Industry

The hearing process is dynamic. It is a give-and-take situation in which the legislators interact with individuals and representatives of interest groups. The dialogue is often lively, and it can lead into unexpected areas. For example, the testimony of an industry representative led to some general and barbed remarks from Brademas about the relationship between industry and the regulatory agencies.

In testifying as a representative of the forest-products industry Dr. Casey E. Westell, Jr., proposed that primary industries, such as forestry and mining, be significantly represented on the advisory committee that would be established for the Environmental Education Act. As precedent he cited the McIntyre–Stennis Act of 1962, whereby it was directed that an advisory committee for forestry research be composed of one-half industry representatives: He said:

> Previously, industry advisory groups were established, altered, abolished and considered at the whim of the administrative agencies. They were so handled that they constituted a "rubber stamp" for agency plans.

Brademas disagreed vehemently:

> From my observation around this town, that is 100 percent wrong, it is the other way around. . . . You can take a whole variety of regulatory agencies in the United States, and I think that what is causing as much concern on the part of so many people in this country is that the regulatory agencies have been captured by the industries that they are supposed to regulate. . . . We write an environmental education program, and then we turn it over to the polluters. I don't understand that.

The Congressman said he was not opposed to industry representation on the council, but that:

> We have to be very careful, not only to be as pure as we can be, but to appear to be pure, if we are going to have the public confidence in the integrity of the programs that are authorized under this bill.

Ecopornography

Industry was involved less directly in the testimony of an advertising man, Jerry Mander, who was also director of Friends of the Earth. Mander's testimony was an indictment of industry's efforts to promote its own image by indicating that it was committed to solving the problems of environmental decay. Mander said one of the tasks of environmental education would be to counter the misinformation produced by the image-conscious industrial concerns, because "God save us, advertising men have discovered ecology." Mander's testimony made clear to the legislators and their staffs that the issue involved in environmental education is a broad one of information in all its forms.

He denigrated advertising campaigns such as that of the Shell Oil Company, which showed "how they saved the lives of a lot of fish by not polluting things as much as they had been," and said the danger is that people will relax and think everything is being taken care of. "Then," he said, "we will have lost their attention."

Mander said industry is spending a billion dollars a year "putting out this stuff," and if conservation organizations paid 1 percent of that amount, "a large part of the country could be educated to understand the difference between ecological messages and . . . 'ecopornography'."

OUTCOME OF THE HEARINGS

During the course of the hearings the legislators heard many suggestions for improving and expanding the bill. The next step was to incorporate some of these suggestions into the language of the legislation.

First, Margaret Mead had recommended that a section be added for getting grant money into the hands of small volunteer groups that would not have the staff or the expertise to prepare exhaustive program proposals. This could be done through the distribution of small amounts, or "mini-grants." She said:

> The way we have got government grants set up at present, you take two months off to write the proposal for the grant.

She suggested that the grant program be simplified, in order

> To get different kinds and sizes of communities into this, and different community forces. . . . And I think mini-grants, with a minimum amount of red tape and professional expertise and jargon, are one way of approaching this.

Garett De Bell, among others, made a similar argument for a simplified funding process for:

The small, unestablished group, the group which has
no auditor because it has no regular sources of funds
. . . the group, in fact, which laid the groundwork of
public concern for this hearing.

In the Environmental Education Act this idea was translated into a section on "Small Grants," which specified that
nonprofit groups with small staffs but innovative ideas
could submit one- to two-page proposals requesting up to
$10,000 to conduct seminars and conferences "especially
for adult and community groups." This placed them in a
position to compete with larger organizations wise in the
art of grantsmanship.

A second contribution was the inclusion of a new project
category—planning outdoor ecological study centers—for
which the National Audubon Society was largely responsible. The Society had pioneered in this area and at that
time was operating several "educational nature centers"
across the country. As the Society's president, Elvis Stahr,
testified, these centers provided "learning experiences" for
children and at the same time served to train teacher-
naturalists. He said the Society had helped plan dozens of
similar centers around the country and at least two abroad,
and that "the need for many, many more is, I think, obvious to all who are concerned with the subject matter of
this bill."

Thirdly, several of the students who appeared before the
Brademas subcommittee stressed the importance of having
students on the Advisory Council. While students had not
been excluded in the original version, neither was it mandatory that they be included. The wording of the final act
was explicit. It specified that "the Council shall consist of
not less than three ecologists and three students." (Other
witnesses had also proposed that ecologists be included.)

It was so unusual to include students in such a committee that this provision was the only source of congressional opposition when the bill came up for a floor vote.

Further, the original bill had no specific provision for funding. This matter was purposefully left open in order to get suggestions, especially from the Administration, on how much money would be appropriate. Brademas asked Allen what would be a reasonable amount of money for a five-year period. The Commissioner promised to send in a "ball-park figure," and this placed the amount at $15 million for fiscal year* 1972, and $25, $35, and $40 million, respectively for the next three fiscal years. Allen also told the Senate subcommittee that he would request $15 million specifically for environmental-education activities in FY 1972 under legislation already in effect. The final version of the bill contained the authorization of $5 million for FY 1971, $15 million for FY 1972, and $25 million for FY 1973.

The final major change was to include a subsection giving a definition of environmental education. The Act says it is:

> . . . the educational process dealing with man's relationship with his natural and man-made surroundings, and includes the relation of population, pollution, resource allocation and depletion, conservation, transportation, technology, and urban and rural planning to the total human environment.

The hearings brought out that it was essential to stipulate that the environment is both the world of nature and the world fashioned by the activities of man. Although it

---

* A fiscal year begins on July 1 and ends on the following June 30. For example, FY 1971 began on July 1, 1970, and ended on June 30, 1971.

was not further specified in the language of the bill, the hearings also made clear the type of educational process that would comprise environmental education. That process was action-oriented, and it envisioned increasing environmental awareness and providing the skills, knowledge, and motivation required to solve environmental problems.

The hearings on the Environmental Education Act were not perfunctory. They served to educate the legislators and their staffs on what the national policy and program in this area should be, and they resulted in changing some of the ideas of the original bill. The hearings were special in the wide range of participants and the quality of their testimony, which dealt with subjects from the concrete to the very abstract, and in their physical bracketing of the nation, from New York to San Francisco and Los Angeles. Their effect, besides the direct impact on the congressmen and the bill itself, was to serve notice that Congress was serious about the legislation and that environmental education was a legitimate issue for a new national policy.

ANOTHER LOOK AT THE STRATEGY

With the hearings completed, it was time for the congressional sponsors to take another look at their overall plans for passing the bill. The high degree of congressional involvement with the bill was already apparent. The Administration had officially endorsed it but was not expected to give much support. Although Commissioner Allen was solidly behind the legislation, he had little clout in the hierarchy of the Nixon Administration. Anyway, shortly after he had testified on the bill before the Senate, he was unceremoniously dismissed for criticizing the Cambodian incursion of May 1970. With Allen gone the chances for Administration support faded.

The hearings were finished by the end of May, which was less than six months after the bill was introduced. However, scarcely another six months lay ahead until the congressional elections in November, with Congress adjourning for one month in mid-October. When Congress reconvened in November, it would be in a lame-duck session, and forecasting legislative activities during that time would be nearly impossible. In addition, Brademas was up for reelection, and there was always the possibility, although remote, that he would be defeated. By the time the hearings were finished, Senator Ralph Yarborough, (D–Tex.), Chairman of the Senate Labor and Public Welfare Committee, had already been defeated in his state's Democratic primary, and consequently, would lose his seat in Congress at the end of the year. A major question was whether or not he would take action on new legislation pending before the committee during his final months.

In general, a lame-duck Congress might pass few pieces of legislation because the power of those defeated tends to diminish and the fate of bills within their scope of authority is less predictable.

Therefore, failure to pass the bill before the elections could greatly complicate matters. The year 1970 was the second and therefore the last session of the Ninety-first Congress, and the bill had to pass before final adjournment or be reintroduced again in the Ninety-second Congress. This would mean that the bill would have to go through the entire legislative process again, when much of the interest and momentum that had been generated would be dissipated. Also, during the next session the timeliness of the bill might be lessened.

Because of the pressure of time the strategy dictated that the bill be moved as quickly as possible through the respective committees, onto the floor for an initial vote, into conference for reconciliation of differences, and back to the floor for final confirmation. This called for a maximum of cooperation between Brademas and Nelson and their staffs to allow them to take advantage of all the opportunities that might become available to speed the passage of the bill.

4

The Legislative Process and the Executive

THE OFFICE OF EDUCATION

THE MAKING of the bill into a law involved direct interaction with the Executive Branch because the proposed
legislation would create a new program within the Office
of Education in the Department of Health, Education and
Welfare. Although Congress was the initiator and prime
mover of the bill, environmental education activities had
already gotten under way in the Office of Education several
months before the bill was introduced, and they served at
the staff level to stimulate more interest on the part of
Congressmen.

Interest in the legislative branch in turn sparked more
activity in the Office of Education. While no official relationship existed between the two branches of government
until the hearings were held on the bill, the back-and-forth
communication by staff members on both sides, in addition

to the expanding activities of OE spurred on by the Commissioner of Education, helped to prepare the way for introducing the bill and for taking the remaining steps of the legislative process.

During the summer of 1969 an Office of Education employee, George E. Lowe, and Special Assistant to the Commissioner of Education, Logan H. Sallada, Jr., began to express their interest in environmental education. Through their efforts a group of 18 student interns working at OE were encouraged to form a summer task force on the environment. This was one of several OE student task forces that studied subjects such as drug abuse and reading problems. Under OE guidance the interns embarked on several ambitious projects. They held a seminar on the concept of environmental education, set up a display outside the Commissioner's door on an experimental inner-city environmental education program, and produced a documentary film on pollution in Washington, D.C., called "Crisis in the Capital: When Will We Ever Learn?"

The most important contribution of the task force was to conduct a survey on the potential of the Office of Education for incorporating environmental education into its activities. By mid-September the survey had been completed, and most of the students were back in college. When the results were pulled together, the Office of Education had its first body of information on environmental education possibilities at the federal level.

After the summer, two Office of Education personnel and a couple of student interns continued on as an ad hoc environmental education staff. From September on the staff was busy drumming up interest for environmental education, and in December they sent Commissioner of Education Allen a memo describing environmental education and stressing the need for OE to take a leadership role in the new field. They also listed specific recommendations on how this could be done.

On December 12 Commissioner Allen responded favorably to their approach in a memorandum that said:

> I am more than delighted with your fine memo on OE's inherent leadership role in ecological/environmental education. Your recommendations are excellent and I would like to discuss them with you as soon as possible. For a starter, I accept your suggestion that I make a major speech on this subject in the near future. An excellent opportunity for this would be the meeting of the American Council of Learned Societies on January 23.

Shortly thereafter they gave him a briefing on the potential of environmental education, and he was favorably impressed.

On January 23 the Commissioner delivered his speech. It was entitled "Education for Survival," and it indicated the priority he gave this new approach to education. He said:

> It is a matter of urgent necessity that we develop in both young and old an understanding of the society in which they live—an increasingly urbanized society with all the problems that this creates. We need to develop ecological studies designed to make everyone aware of the fragile and interacting relationships of land, air and water—and to give new understandings of the eco-concepts—that must govern the develop-

ment of society, encompassing the demands of increasing urbanization.

Allen said education was the key to human survival because it was the only means of equipping citizens with the knowledge and understanding they would need to make the choices and take the action necessary to reverse the trend of a deteriorating environment. New laws and regulations were important, but an effective response would call for understanding on the part of individual citizens about ways of reducing the tensions between man, his technology, and the environment. He also said it was the responsibility of the government to take the lead in encouraging the growth of public understanding, concern, and participation. He further announced that it would be necessary to create an environmental-education-studies staff to coordinate existing programs, redirect existing resources, and plan new programs and activities in the Office of Education. This was a firm political commitment by the Commissioner to the cause of environmental education, and it triggered a series of events helpful to the legislation during the next few weeks.

The studies staff Allen referred to in his speech was officially created from the existing informal staff on February 9, 1970. The Commissioner also established a Task Force on Environmental/Ecological Education, which was directed by Logan H. Sallada, Jr. In a memorandum issued that day the Commissioner said:

On January 23, 1970, I spoke before the American Council of Learned Socities concerning a . . . national priority in education. My remarks entitled, "Education for Survival" envisioned a commitment to a concept of environmental/ecological education which cuts across the entire continuum of education. The Office of Education commitment to EEE will be given the highest priority. To begin its immediate implementation, I am establishing an Environmental Education Task Force comprised initially of OE personnel: but one which will eventually include representatives from other agencies concerned with EEE.

The environmental education staff became the supporting staff for the task force, which was composed of 25 representatives from the major offices and bureau in OE. The representatives were expected to devote 50 percent of their time to the task force. The purpose of the task force was to identify potential resources within OE for undertaking programs in environmental education, to act as an advocate for the new concept, and to provide a sounding board for ideas.

Allen's decision looked good in theory. If environmental education cut across all major programs, it was sensible to have representatives from those programs form such a study group and to ensure that they devote a considerable portion of their time to the effort. Also he saw the potential for dynamic interaction between the various programs of OE to create other environmental education efforts that could be sustained after the task force was dissolved. Allen planned to use his regular monthly meetings with bureau chiefs and office directors to find out what each was doing in carrying out the recommendations of the task force. In a sense he could use this as an experiment to see on a small scale how well he could coordinate the activities of his entire office.

In practice, many of the members could not or would not spend half their time on work that was in addition to their regular tasks. Their regular work load did not diminish by 50 per cent in most cases and extra time was hard to find. Also, the understandable tendency was to protect the interests of the office each member represented rather than to determine the best possible courses for OE to follow. Finally, like other large bureaucracies the Office of Education has historically had difficulty in dealing with processes or new concepts that overlap conventional lines of organization.

THE EXECUTIVE BRANCH

Two factors weighed heavily against Executive Branch support for new legislative authority in environmental education.

First, Commissioner Allen did not visualize environmental education as a discrete program but as a goal toward which funding from his major ongoing programs should be directed. It was a form of educational reform representing a change in the style of teaching, and its purposes could be accomplished by redirecting funds under existing legislative authority. Therefore, no new legislation was required.

Second, the Nixon administration's policy did not favor the proliferation of new programs, and under the proposed legislation a new "categorical" environmental education program, with its own separate budget, would be created in the Office of Education. A categorical program is one that appears as a separate item in the federal budget, which gives Congress the opportunity to maintain accountability on the program through the appropriations and oversight functions, denying the Executive Branch, for example, the flexibility to shift funds out of that program without permission from Congress.

The Republican Administration, more explicitly than previous administrations, had decided as a policy to oppose new categorical programs, because it felt that the Democratic administrations of Kennedy and Johnson, as well as the Democratic-controlled Congresses, had created too many new programs to manage effectively. From an Executive Branch standpoint there was a need to consolidate wherever possible to improve efficiency, particularly in the Department of HEW, the largest domestic Agency in the federal government.

On several occasions the President made this policy position clear in speeches, addresses, and messages. The most succinct statement of this position appears in his Special Message to the Congress on Consolidation of Federal Assistance Programs. President Nixon said:

> Under our present fragmented system, each one of a group of closely related categorical grants is encumbered with its own individual array of administrative and technical requirements. This unnecessarily complicated the planning process: it discourages comprehensive planning; it requires multiple bookkeeping both by the federal agencies and by state and local governments.

There is no ambiguity in this policy statement, and the Administration took a firm approach to carrying it out.

Allen viewed environmental education in light of these factors. Eventually he found it nearly impossible to generate this innovative activity in an inertia-prone bureaucracy and began to look differently on the proposed legislation. The bill's passage might give him more leverage to administer environmental education affairs. The task force proved to be ineffective, and he allowed it to dissolve on April 30 as originally scheduled. However, the Environmental Education Studies Staff remained on as an entity of questionable official status.

The House hearings were scheduled for April 21. Commissioner Allen, who was in sympathy with the purposes of the bill, was informed that the Office of Management and Budget (OMB), which ordinarily decides on an administration's position on proposed legislation unless the decision is made in the White House, would not give the legislation official Administration support. OMB was carrying out the Administration's policy by opposing the creation of a new categorical program.

When the Commissioner testified before the House subcommittee he said the Office already had sufficient authority to support environmental education, was already supporting it, and intended to expand its efforts. The statement defended the official line, but it was apparent that the Commissioner was disappointed with the Executive Branch's official stance and that he had no choice but to speak out against the bill. Brademas was not happy either, but he knew of the Commissioner's personal and official commitments to environmental education, and in the discussion period that followed the delivery of the prepared statement (which had to be cleared by OMB), Brademas set the stage for Allen to state his position more accurately:

> MR. BRADEMAS: As I indicated at the outset of these hearings this morning, by having quoted from your address of January to the American Council of

Learned Societies, which I thought was a splendid address, I have no questions in my own mind of your personal commitment for the idea, and the need for federal support of environmental education, but I do have profound misgivings about the support given by the Administration to efforts in this field.

COMMISSIONER ALLEN: Well, I think, Mr. Chairman, that your comments about our statement that no additional authority is needed, and, therefore, this bill is not necessary in order to do something, is wrong, because whether we have this legislation or not, we are in a position and plan indeed to take advantage of existing legislation. We plan to move ahead in environmental education.

These were not the words of a man who opposed the Act.

That evening the Commissioner arrived at the University of Wisconsin at Madison to participate in the beginning of the school's Earth Day activities. In a speech entitled "Environmental Ecological Education—For the Survival of a Human Society" he praised environmental education and pledged "that the U.S. Office of Education will take a positive, innovative position in the forefront of this race between education and catastrophe." Following the speech he was surprised with embarrassing questions about his public testimony earlier that day, when he had announced the Administration's opposition to the Environmental Education Act. The Brademas and Nelson staffs had planted the questions with university officials and student leaders by telephone calls immediately after the hearings in order to put pressure on Allen and the Executive Branch to reverse the official position on the bill.

Environmental education was not a passion with the Commissioner, nor was it simply a hobby. Allen believed in the merits of this approach to education and felt at this point that the Environmental Education Act called for such a small program that there should be no reason to have to speak out against it at the upcoming Senate hearings, thus implying that the Administration would not support innovative steps to help resolve the environmental issue. He felt that would tend to make the Administration's stated commitment to improving the nation's environment on a long-term basis somewhat hollow and superficial.

As has been mentioned in Chapter 3, the Administration did change its stance to support the bill. Although Allen had very little access to or rapport with the White House, he felt strongly enough about this matter to bypass OMB and go directly to John Ehrlichman, Nixon's foremost domestic advisor on the White House staff. Allen said that he would not testify against the Environmental Education Act at the Senate hearings, and if the Administration continued to oppose the bill, someone else would have to testify. To Allen's surprise Ehrlichman did not know about the bill, and he gave the Commissioner the green light to announce the Administration's support of it.

On May 19 Allen appeared before the Senate Subcommittee on Education, he recommended that the authority to administer the bill rest with the Secretary of HEW and not with the Commissioner of Education, as the bill prescribed. This type of change might prove difficult for Congress to accept. Spreading the authority of a bill with relatively small funding limits across such a large number of offices and agencies would present the legislative branch with a problem in maintaining adequate accountability

over it. Therefore, this move could have appeared to congressmen as a means of supporting the bill but ensuring
that it would not survive in the bureaucracy.

On the other hand, the idea of environmental education
covered a broad subject area and did generate interest
within other parts of HEW. This was borne out by the fact
that Dr. John J. Hanlon, Acting Administrator of the Environmental Health Service, accompanied Commissioner
Allen when he testified. The Acting Administrator's pre-
sence was an indication that the interest in this piece of
legislation went beyond the Office of Education.

If Congress were to ensure that the program became a
reality, it would have to make a decision between a depart-
ment-wide program and one of a specific activity placed in
OE. The final choice was to opt for a program to be administered by the Office of Education. It was fortunate that
the decision was made this way, because the high-level
support Allen had given the bill was to disappear when he
was fired by the President a few weeks later.

Allen's bold decision to go to the White House on the
Environmental Education Act was followed by his open
criticism of the Administration several days later, when
he was speaking before OE employees on current events.
The discussion covered a wide variety of topics and was
followed by a question-and-answer period. In one of the
final questions Allen was asked to give his views on the
President's decision to commit American troops to land
battle in Cambodia, for the first time in the long Vietnam
war. Instead of the bland reply prepared by his staff the
Commissioner read a statement he had written the night
before, which said:

> I find it difficult to understand the rationale for the
> necessity of the move into Cambodia as a means of

supporting and hastening the withdrawal from Viet Nam—a withdrawal that I feel must be accomplished as soon as possible.

What concerns me most now is what our responsibility is in dealing with the disastrous effects that this action has had on education throughout the country and on the confidence of millions of concerned citizens in their government.

Twelve days later the Secretary of HEW wrote to Allen that he had been directed to ask for his resignation from the Administration. On the next day the Commissioner tendered his resignation in a terse letter to the President.

5

The Legislative Process and Congress

THE ENVIRONMENTAL Education Act was moving through Congress during a period of growing congressional disenchantment with the intentions of the Executive Branch to carry out public law. In the area of federal education bills monumental programs had been passed in the spate of domestic legislation that followed the landslide Democratic Presidential victory in 1964, including the Elementary and Secondary Education and Higher Education acts. By 1970 Congress was beginning to take a look at what had been accomplished. Many of the members and staffs of the Education subcommittees in both houses were not overly pleased with what the Office of Education had done with its legislative authority. They were becoming increasingly doubtful of OE's competency to carry out the intent of Congress as it was embodied in the education legislation and increasingly aware of a need for Congress to exert its constitutional prerogatives. This would involve more explicitly structured legislation to allow for closer oversight of the administration of federal programs.

The history of the Environmental Education Act was embroiled in this question of the credibility of the Executive Branch, both during and after the bill was enacted into law. The sponsors on both sides of Congress felt that it might not be possible to trust the Executive Branch to abide by the mandate expressed in the legislation. In the Senate this concern was manifested in the inclusion of an organizational amendment directing the means by which the Office of Education would have to administer the program.

On the Executive side OE officials and their staffs firmly maintained that their statements had been in harmony with their intentions, that the inertia of the bureaucracy was the real stumbling block to faster and more effective implementation of the legislation. At any rate the Administration's record of initial opposition and later reluctance to support the bill cast some doubt upon OE's willingness to give the program the priority Congress intended.

THE INTERNAL STRUCTURING AMENDMENT

While the bill was still in committee and before the Senate hearings took place, congressional distrust was expressed in an amendment to the bill introduced on the floor by Senator Pell, calling for the creation of an Office of Environmental Education to be placed within the immediate office of the Commissioner and to be directed by a GS-17-

level civil servant. The Office would administer its own
program and coordinate all environmental education
activities within OE.

It was simply a matter of chance that this amendment
was offered to the Environmental Education Act. Such a
move from the Senate subcommittee had been coming for
some time.

The issue of where and how to draw the line between
the legislation and administration of programs (i.e., the
separation of powers concept) was raised in a Senate
Labor and Public Welfare Committee report published on
January 21 of that year entitled "Elementary and Secondary Education Amendments of 1969." The report stated:

> Decisions with respect to the organizational structure
> of administrative agencies in general, and the Office
> of Education in particular, are generally considered
> by this committee to be properly left to the agency
> head. In the case of the Office of Education, this Com-
> mittee has made only one exception to this general
> rule—the statutory Bureau for the Education of the
> Handicapped. That exception was legislated only
> because there was apparent confusion respecting, and
> even the lack of sensitivity to, the education of handi-
> capped children within the Office of Education.

It further hinted that future specific moves in this area
could be expected from the Senate committee:

> The Committee does not wish to legislate the struc-
> ture of the Bureau of Elementary and Secondary
> Education: however, when disorganization and con-
> fusion endanger the effectiveness of programs estab-
> lished by law and cause uncertainty at the local level,

legislation to provide guidance or direction may be necessitated.

The internal-structuring amendment proposed for the Environmental Education Act was a test case of this pronouncement that Congress would cross the traditional separation of powers boundaries in order to legislate more effectively and to maintain the system of checks and balances.

The change embodied in the amendment could not become a part of the bill until after the Senate hearings, and the existence of the amendment apparently was not noticed by the policy-level administrators at the Office of Education, because Commissioner Allen did not respond to it in his testimony. Shortly thereafter the Executive Branch realized the implications of the amendment, especially since it was introduced by the subcommittee chairman and would therefore probably appear in the final Senate version of the bill. The battle was on over whether or not the section should be included in the bill.

In addition to causing immediate problems, the new wording was later incorporated in the Act and served as a model for a move two years later to structure several of the major authorities within the Office of Education. The language of this later proposal was not adopted, but it served as a warning not to move programs around within the Office of Education without prior congressional approval. Congress was not opposed in principle to the consolidation of programs or to the internal transfer of funds from one program to another, but it wanted to know what was planned since such moves would affect programs already legislated, and Congress insisted on officially approving the plans. The Executive Branch preferred an after-the-fact notification.

While the amendment strengthened the bill from a congressional standpoint, it increased the potential difficulty of passing and perhaps implementing it. The amendment could draw fire from the Administration, which might consider it an intrusion on its constitutional prerogatives. The tension between the two branches of government over this amendment, low-keyed at first, continued through the remainder of the legislative phase and into the appropriations and oversight phases and is still a live issue as this is written.

SUBCOMMITTEE ACTIONS

Following the hearings the Environmental Education Act was ready to be amended and reported out of the subcommittees and full committees having jurisdiction over the bill in both houses. The bill had to be voted on favorably at each of these two levels before it could be brought to the floor for a vote.

The Nelson and Brademas staffs, with the assistance of the EE Staff, would each have to prepare a revised version of the bill incorporating any recommendations from the hearings and from their subsequent discussions that would improve and refine it. Each staff would also write the first drafts of the report that would accompany the legislation to the floor. The drafts would then be carefully reviewed by the bill's sponsors before they would be ready for the subcommittee to consider.

The report contains a bill's legislative history, provides a section-by-section analysis of it, and discusses the intent of Congress on a broader and more philosophical level than can be included in its practical language.

The next step is "markup", which takes place at a closed meeting of the subcommittee called an executive session. In the markup process the new draft of the bill is explained and debated. At this point amendments other than those already incorporated in the draft are considered and can be adopted through a majority vote.

On June 24, less than four months before Congress was to adjourn for the November elections, the House Select Subcommittee on Education reported out the Environmental Education Act to the full committee for its consideration. This amended version reflected many of the recommendations made during the hearings (see Chapter 3) along with the subcommittee's decision as to which official in the Executive Branch should receive the authority to administer the program.

In the House version the bill was amended to give the Secretary of HEW the program responsibility, in consonance with the Administration's request, and the report recommended that the Secretary delegate the authority to the Commissioner of Education. Brademas subcommittee members were not overly concerned about this change, because they had good reason to believe that the delegation of authority would naturally take place.

On the Senate side the Subcommittee on Education reported out its version of the bill unanimously on July 30, one month after the House subcommittee had acted and two and a half months before Congress would adjourn. This version did not incorporate any of the changes made in the House but did contain the Pell amendment calling for the internal structuring of the Office of Education and placing prime responsibility on the shoulders of the Commissioner. Also, it authorized funding ceilings well below those of its House counterpart.

The two new bills contained significant differences that

would have to be reconciled in conference before a final version could be enacted. First, the amended Senate bill created an Office of Environmental Education headed by a director at a high level in the Civil Service. The second major difference was in the two sets of authorization figures. The House subcommittee authorized a total of $45 million for three fiscal years, including $5 million for that current fiscal year, while the Senate bill authorized $16 million for the same period of time. An important distinction was that the Senate bill authorized no funds for the current fiscal year.

The lower authorization figure of the Senate bill helped to tone down the controversy that might arise over the organizational change. The Senate sponsors felt that even if the bill met opposition, it could still be passed in a floor vote. House sponsors, with a less controversial bill, were even more confident of a favorable decision. Later, when differences would have to be resolved in conference, the higher authorization levels from the House bill could be retained along with the mandate to create an Office of Environmental Education. The compromise bill reported out of conference might be stronger than either of the original versions.

COMMITTEE ACTION

With a virtual lack of opposition to the bill in either subcommittee, the sponsors anticipated little difficulty at the full committee level. The real problem in moving the bill through the committee to the floor for a vote would be to get the measure onto the agenda for action. Three factors were involved.

The first was the competition for time with other bills that were being pushed by other committee members and their staffs. These pressures were intensifying due to the short amount of time remaining before preelection adjournment.

The second factor related to the possibility of a shift in the control of Congress from the Democrats to the Republicans. All representatives and one-third of the senators are up for reelection every even year. In November 1970, 25 of the 33 senators whose terms were expiring were Democrats, and 17 of those were northern and western liberals, many of whom had been brought into the Senate or kept in office as a result of Johnson's smashing triumph over Goldwater in 1964. With so many Democratic positions on the line and with the close split between the majority and minority parties in the Senate—57 Democrats and 43 Republicans—the Republicans had a better-than-average chance, numerically, of taking over the Senate.

At the same time off-year elections historically have not been fruitful for the party in the White House, and off-year elections during wartime (the Vietnam War was a major issue then) have been even less productive. The only exception to this since 1942 was in the 1962 election, when favorable public reaction to Kennedy's handling of the Cuban missile crisis in October of that year helped prevent the Republicans from making gains.

In spite of the fact that the Republicans were a minority party in the White House in an off-year election during a time of war, President Nixon made a strong bid to gain control of the Senate and, to a lesser extent, the House. Because of the upcoming political battle the Administration had a greater tendency to regard Democratic moves in Congress as partisan efforts. It was possible that the

Republicans might not be eager to see the bill reported out favorably or enacted into law. *

Third, the scheduling of the Environmental Education Act for a committee markup was complicated by the uncertainty of whether or not the defeated Chairman of the Senate Committee on Labor and Public Welfare, Ralph Yarborough, would want to schedule an executive session on the bill. Representative Carl Perkins, Chairman of the House Committee on Education and Labor, was running for reelection in a relatively safe district in the state of Kentucky. It was more predictable that he would be an active chairman during the preelection period.

On the other hand, the bill had a strong hearing record, and the environmental issue was timely. The House committee reported the bill out in late July with no changes and with nearly unanimous support. The Senate committee took up the bill about one month later and unanimously reported it out on September 9, also with no changes.

FLOOR ACTION

The Chairman of the House committee became floor manager for the bill, which meant he would lead the debate in favor of the measure and attempt to obtain a favorable

* The results of the elections were not unexpected despite the President's putting so much of his prestige on the line. Before the elections, the Senate was divided 57 to 43 in favor of the Democrats. The elections resulted in a net shift of only two seats to the Republicans, narrowing the margin to 55 to 45, but the Democrats retained control of the Senate. The shift in the House followed the historical pattern, and the party in the White House lost strength. The Democrats made a net gain of nine seats.

vote. The selection of a floor manager depends upon the committee involved. He is usually the majority-party member who is the author or chief sponsor of the bill or the chairman of the subcommittee or committee that reported it out.

The bill was called up on August 3, which was the first Monday of the month. The day of the month regarding House action is very significant, because on two days of each month (the first and third Mondays) certain rules of the House can be suspended and the powerful Rules Committee bypassed. In the House each piece of legislation, except for appropriation bills, is given a ruling by the Rules Committee, which must pass on it favorably before it can be considered for passage. On the first and third Mondays this requirement can be circumvented.

After receiving the required recognition by the Speaker of the House, the bill was called up for floor action. Bills handled in this manner must have a two-thirds, rather than a simple majority vote to pass. Because the bill had almost no opposition, the sponsors felt confident in invoking this procedure. It would be dangerous to bypass the Rules Committee with a controversial bill, because a two-thirds majority would be very difficult to get.

Representative Ogden Reid (D–N.Y.), one of the four original sponsors, read into the record a letter from the HEW Secretary stating the terms the Administration was placing on its support for the measure. Secretary Elliot Richardson had written:

> While we do not feel that additional legislative authority is needed to carry out the objectives of H.R. 14753, we are in accord with its objectives and do not

oppose its enactment. Further, the bill as amended by
the Education and Labor Committee places the authority for environmental education in the hands of
the secretary, and makes several other changes which
remove our technical objections to the original version.

This meant the sponsors had prior assurance that the bill
would not meet opposition from the Administration.

Yet there was opposition to the bill on the floor. Representative Earl F. Landgrebe (R–Ind.) thought that the
$45-million authorization was inflationary, but he also
spoke out specifically against the section that gave the
Secretary of HEW authority to appoint at least three
students to the Advisory Council. He said:

Do we politicians feel that we must have the student
interest, particularly since we lowered the voting age
to 18, and that we ought to have more student voting
for our party or the other party? If so, this is all good
and fine, but we are talking about management, about
the operation of the U.S. Government.

Of course, I am a new member here, but investigation reveals that this is the first time we have designated that three students shall be members of a very
important committee, of a committee which, if this
bill passes will be spending some $45 million of the
taxpayers' dollars during the next three years.

Brademas replied:

I fear that my friend from Indiana is somewhat mis-
taken if he suggested that the bill contemplated

students would be teaching teachers. There is a provision in the bill for membership of at least three
students on the 21-member advisory committee which
is only an advisory committee and not the administering body for carrying out the purposes of the bill.

It was ironic that this was the only significant opposition
to the Environmental Education Act, in light of the strong
case that had been made for student involvement in environmental education during the hearings.

When the yeas and nays were asked, the Environmental
Education Act was approved by a vote of 289 to 28, a
margin far greater than the required two-thirds majority.

On the Senate side the Majority Leader called up the
Environmental Education Act on September 21. It was
early on a Monday morning, and Senator Nelson, who had
arranged for this to be done, was still on an airplane en
route from Milwaukee to Washington. He was behind
schedule and would not be present to lead the floor debate. Because the Senate operates under more flexible
rules than the House, Nelson's staff aide could try to
locate another Senator to serve as floor manager. House
procedures are more formal, and in a similar situation the
vote would most likely be deferred for another day.

After a twenty-minute flurry of phone calls the aide
contacted the administrative assistant of Senator Harold
Hughes (D–Iowa), who said he would get his boss down
to the floor of the Senate to fill in for Nelson.

A few minutes later Hughes was in the Senate chamber.
He acknowledged Nelson's unavoidable absence and inserted into the *Congressional Record* the statement the
Wisconsin Senator would have presented. The statement
said:

It will not be possible to develop broad environmental policies until we totally reexamine the relationships between ourselves, nature and the world
we have created. Man must come to understand that
he is part of a delicate balance, and if he degrades,
diminishes, wastes or misuses vital resources, he
threatens his survival and that of all living things.

To change attitudes and to develop a conscious ethic
that says man must not destroy and despoil his environment will require a major educational effort, for
education is the only way to influence beliefs in a
democratic society.

Hughes was on the parent committee and was to some
extent familiar with the bill. Using arguments prepared by
Nelson's staff aide, he voiced his own support of the bill
and led the debate.

Several other members rose in support of the proposed
legislation but none expressed criticism of it. When a roll-
call vote was asked, the result was 64 yeas and 0 nays.
Despite the implications of the internal-structuring
amendment the bill had received unanimous Senate support.

CONFERENCE ACTION: THE MINI-CONFERENCE

The bill was now ready for conference. Without a reconciliation of differences between the two versions it could
not become law.

Conferences are conducted by members from the committees having jurisdiction over the bill in both houses and

include a representative number of congressmen from both parties. The conference committees are usually composed of the bill's leading proponents and, when there are any, its opponents. The conferees must come up with an amended bill that removes the differences between the Senate and House versions. In some cases this means merely adopting a part of one bill that doesn't appear in the other; in others, such as instances of differing levels of authorization, a compromise might have to be struck between the high and low levels. If the conferees cannot agree, the bill is frozen and it cannot be reported out of conference. If they do reach agreement, the compromise measure along with a conference report is sent back to each house, where it is scheduled for an "accept-or-reject-all" majority vote; conference bills cannot be amended from the floor. However, versions rejected by either or both houses can be sent back to conference with hopes that differences over controversial sections will be ironed out. A conference can be avoided altogether if the House and Senate versions of a measure are identical after initial passage. In this case the two versions are considered as one bill, and enaction into law depends only upon the President's approval.

This option was considered before markup by the sponsors of the Environmental Education Act and their staffs. The House version could have contained the internal-structuring amendment, and the Senate bill could have incorporated the House amendments including the higher authorization ceilings. With minor changes in wording the two bills would have been identical and would have had to pass the House and Senate only once before being sent to the President for his signature.

Several problems were involved with this approach.

First, if congressmen perceived that a bill was being moved too quickly, they might be suspicious that this was a deliberate attempt to hide some controversial feature and decide to slow the process down for scrutiny and debate on the measure.

Second, it would be difficult for the House or the Senate to justify accepting changes to the bill that had not been brought up in its subcommittee hearings or in amendments formally offered before it. For example, the House subcommittee would have had difficulty in justifying the inclusion of the organizational change embodied in the Senate version because nothing was mentioned about that amendment during its hearings, and the Senate subcommittee would have been saddled with a similar problem on an amendment such as the mini-grant section, which was discussed only during the House hearings.

Third, a bill passed through Congress without a conference and subsequent report would have a weaker legislative history and might therefore have a lower priority and less chance for passage. The sponsors saw a need to take shortcuts when and where possible but not to the extent of jeopardizing the bill's future.

The legislative history of the Environmental Education Act did not indicate that any major controversies would arise during the conference. In fact, there was so little disagreement on the measure within Congress that the major proponents from both houses decided to hold a *nearly unprecedented* "mini-conference," in which only the respective staffs would participate, rather than a formal conference, in which the Congressmen themselves must take part. The purpose of this move was to save time; the disadvantage involved was that the bill's legislative record would be weakened. The legislators would not file a conference report, and their final floor statements would have to take its place.

With only weeks remaining before adjournment, the key House and Senate staff members met to come up with a final version. The result of this informal conference was that the major amendments of both bills were incorporated in the final version. First, it was readily agreed upon that the House measures to clarify and reform the bill would stay in. The mini-grant section stayed, as did the naming of three students and three ecologists to the Advisory Council, the planning of ecological study centers, and the authorizing of $45 million over a three-year period. This funding matter proved to be no problem. On the second major difference between the two bills, the internal-structuring amendment, a compromise was necessary.

The Senate version, which called for an Office of Environmental Education and specified the level of its director, was causing a problem for the Administration and to a lesser extent for Brademas and his staff. The Administration did not want Congress to dictate exactly how the bill would be administered, and the House subcommittee staffers were sympathetic with this position. HEW Secretary Richardson had sent a letter to the House Education and Labor Committee Chairman expressing the Administration's strong opposition to this part of the Act. The Secretary had written:

> Our second concern is with the requirement in S.3151 [Senate version of the Environmental Education Act] which establishes within the Office of Education an Office of Environmental Education, headed by a Director compensated at the GS-17 level. We believe

that this requirement is unnecessary and unwise. It runs counter to the generally accepted principle that the statutory prescription of internal organization of the Executive Branch departments and agencies should be avoided. It mandates one particular approach to administering an educational activity which is new and still evolving and which might suffer from a premature rigidity of structure.

The Administration believed, with good reason, that the congressional purpose violated the separation of powers doctrine. However, the primary concern of the Senate sponsors was not to tell the Executive how to administer a program but to see that a new idea, once translated into legislation, would be implemented along the lines that Congress had prescribed.

After much give-and-take between the staff aides, they were able to agree upon two significant changes. First, the Senate staffers agreed to spell "office of environmental education" in lower-case letters. This meant that the Administration would have more leeway to decide what priority the "office" would have, thereby giving it more flexibility in deciding how many levels beneath the Commissioner the unit might be placed—a fact the Senate staff aides were uneasy about.

Second, they also agreed that the director of the office would no longer have to be a GS-17 (next to the highest level in the regular Civil Service classification) but a civil servant of a ranking *no higher* than a GS-17. This was another significant change because it meant that the Office of Education now had another avenue to downgrade the priority of the program.

The legislators and their staffs felt that watering down

this section was probably necessary because of the Administration's strong opposition to those provisions and the possibility that it would block the measure at the last minute or later resist its implementation.

FINAL FLOOR ACTION

On October 5, ten days before preelection adjournment, the House/Senate compromise was printed up and ready for final passage.

This time a ruling had to be obtained from the House Rules Committee, which meant that Brademas had to convince the Chairman of his committee to appear before the Rules Committee to seek a favorable ruling so that the bill could be brought to the floor for a final vote. With so little time remaining until adjournment and with many other bills before the Chairman for consideration this was a lot to expect. However, a ruling was sought and obtained. The majority and minority leaders in both chambers also had to be contacted to clear the legislation.

On October 13, at 11:05 A.M., the Environmental Education Act passed the House unanimously by voice vote. Brademas had discussed the changes that had been made to the measure since its first passage. He stressed the intent of Congress regarding implementation of the Act:

> It should be noted by officials at the Office of Education that the action by the House in making the changes that I have just described [The Internal-Structuring Amendment] does not indicate that the

house would tolerate burying the new Office of Environmental Education within one of the various bureaus of the Office of Education where it will receive little focus. It is the clear intention of the House that activities in environmental education be coordinated chiefly under the control of the new Office of Environmental Education and that the Office have a prominence within the Office of Education which will insure that it has the authority effectively to carry out the programs authorized by this Act.

I make this point only to assure the Office of Education that in the future review of this program, Congress will exercise diligence to make very certain that the Office of Environmental Education will not become a powerless group located within the sprawling bureaucracy of the Office of Education.

Brademas and his staff then raced to the House engrossing room, where bills are prepared for transmission to the Senate, to help in an effort to speed up the process of verifying that the bill was sent to the Senate exactly as it was passed by the House. With only two days left before adjournment every minute counted, and nothing was left to chance. The startled engrosser remarked to his temporary assistant, "I've worked here for twenty years and I have never seen a Congressman in here before."

One and a half hours later the bill was sent to the Senate. Only three Senators were on the floor at that time, and again Nelson was not there. At that stage the task of ensuring passage could be handled by staff aides. As long as the staff of the minority leader indicated that the measure had been cleared and the majority leader's staff was aware of this, nothing was left to be done. The bill was quickly called up by the senator representing the majority party and passed by unanimous voice vote. Following the complications of the legislative process, the congressional ending was anticlimactic.

Nelson's prepared statement, like that of Brademas, also served in lieu of a conference report to stress the intent of Congress. Nelson asserted:

> The intent is that this office should be located within the immediate Office of the Commissioner. This was the intent of the Senate Subcommittee on Education and the full Committee on Labor and Public Welfare as evidenced in the report of the Senate. This bill passed the Senate unanimously, 64 to 0, and therefore, one could only conclude that the intent of the Senate was identical to the intent of the Committee report.

Both Brademas and Nelson had reason to expect the Executive Branch to continue to fight the legislation even though it had now passed Congress and was on its way to the White House.

PRESIDENTIAL ACTION

With the bill on the desk of the President the legislative battle appeared to be over; it seemed that the stone of Sisyphus could not roll again.

The President could veto the bill, but this was unlikely because of the nearly unanimous votes in both houses, and it would not be hard to muster the two-thirds majorities necessary to override the veto. If the President refused to sign the bill, it would still become law automatically after ten working days.

About one week after final passage of the bill one of the staffers discovered a startling fact: if the President decided not to sign the bill, it would not automatically become law because the President held pocket-veto power during the adournment. Whenever the House adjourns for more than three days, the House Clerk is instructed to receive routine messages but no veto messages from the President. Thus, if the President cannot veto a bill, i.e., send it back to the originating body for reconsideration, he acquires the power of the pocket veto. This applies to all bills identified by a House of Representatives number, and the Environmental Education Act passed Congress the final time with a House number. Normally the pocket veto is associated with adjournments at the end of each session and not with midsession adournments. Upon learning this, the sponsors and their staffs sought ways of indirectly influencing the President to sign the bill. This meant that for the first and only time in the history of the Act significant lobbying efforts were mounted by environmental and educational organizations.

With just hours left before the November elections there was little else Congress could do but hope that the President would sign the bill. The Administration was not at all pleased with the final version of the Environmental Education Act for the reasons stated previously. Therefore, it was not surprising that a few members of the OE and HEW staffs tried to persuade the White House to let this and several other congressionally initiated HEW bills expire. In the final analysis, however, the issue boiled down to whether or not President Nixon could reject a measure that many of his advisors felt the public would consider synonymous with motherhood.

On October 31, 1970, two days before the election, Brademas, campaigning in his district in Indiana, learned from a Chicago newspaper that the President had signed the Environmental Education Act into law on October 30. Nelson and his staff read the news in *The New York Times*. The Act was now Public Law 91–516 (see Appendix 1, PL 91–516).

6

The Appropriations Process

THE FIRST ROUND

WITH THE law on the books, the legislative phase was completed, but the long uphill battle to translate an idea into reality was far from finished. Other important steps would have to follow. The uncertainty at this point was whether the Executive Branch would ask Congress for appropriations to carry out the legislative idea, as a matter of course, or whether Congress would have to take the initiative to make sure that money would be provided. In either case appropriations would be needed to legally commit the Administration to expend these funds only for the purposes specified in the Act.

While the appropriations process occurs in the same sequence as the legislative process, the substance is quite different. It is to determine levels of funding for programs in contrast to creating new programs or modifying and amending the statutory base of existing programs. Appropriations must come after enabling legislation has been passed, authorizing the maximum amount of money that may be spent for one or more fiscal years. The amount actually appropriated can range from nothing upward to the authorized ceiling, but providing no money to implement legislation is equivalent to killing it. The level of funding is indicative of the degree of priority a program is being given by the federal government, and the overall budget is one of the best indicators of the ranking given to federal priorities.

The authorization levels set in the Act provided that a maximum of $5 million could be spent for the fiscal year in which the bill was passed, 1971, but by the time the law was enacted, most avenues for securing the necessary appropriations were already closed. The regular appropriations hearings on the Office of Education budget had been held during the spring of 1970, and the education appropriations bill had become law on August 18—too soon for the Environmental Education Act to be considered. Furthermore, the supplemental-appropriations hearings on Office of Education programs in the House had been completed in September. (A supplemental appropriations bill is a potpourri of additional funding requests for ongoing programs and for newly legislated programs that are considered after the regular appropriations process for specific agencies. Many subject areas are lumped together under one supplemental appropriations bill.) Senate supplemental hearings were still being conducted in late November, and so the best and perhaps the only opportunity for action in FY 1971 to appropriate money for the Environmental Education Act was in the Senate. Passage of the supplemental-appropriations bill under consideration was targeted for the end of the session, and this would almost certainly be the last supplemental enacted before the President announced his budget for the next fiscal year in early January.

If the proponents were to wait for another FY 1971 supplemental, it would probably be too late to get an appropriation for the Environmental Education Act, because there might be no further supplementals, and by then the appropriations subcommittees would be wholly preoccupied with the FY 1972 budget. With the Executive Branch's history of resistance or, at best, grudging support of the legislation, it seemed improbable to the sponsors that the Administration would ask for either a supplemental appropriation for FY 1971 or a regular appropriation for FY 1972 unless Congress successfully initiated an FY 1971 supplemental request in November. A congressionally initiated appropriation for FY 1971 would make it difficult for the Administration to avoid including a funding request for the Act in the forthcoming budget.

In contrast to the legislative process, in which most of the action came from Brademas and his staff, the appropriations process was dominated by Nelson. To take advantage of the supplemental-appropriations bill before the Senate, Nelson wrote Senator Robert C. Byrd (D–W. Va.), Chairman of the Subcommittee on Deficiencies and Supplemental Appropriations, on November 20, requesting that the full $5 million authorization be appropriated for the Act. Nelson said in his letter:

> Already, in large part because of the enthusiasm shown by the federal government and the timeliness of the legislation, the new Office has received un-

solicited proposals totalling in excess of $11 million for this fiscal year. . . .

. . . I request that you consider funding the Act to the authorized ceiling for this fiscal year as part of the supplemental appropriations bill which I understand is due to be reported out of full committee sometime in early to mid-December, 1970.

The chance to hear an Administration response came a few days later. James B. Cardwell, Comptroller of HEW, was before the Byrd Subcommittee testifying in favor of Administration supplemental requests for other programs when Byrd asked him about the Environmental Education Act. Although Cardwell had little advance warning about the Nelson request and the fact that the Senate might include funds for the Act, his response implied that there was a wide difference in the priority that was being given to the Act by the two branches of government. Cardwell stated:

Again I would like to qualify my answer to make it quite clear that we might not ask Congress for any special funding of this program. If we did install the program, per se, it could perhaps be done through reprogramming from other areas.

We do pledge to you that we will give emphasis to this basic subject in keeping with the spirit of what we understand that Act to have intended. The question of whether we later install a special program under that Act or not, we would hold over until 1972.

Cardwell's reply seemed to indicate that it was up to the Executive Branch to decide whether or not to implement the program, even after Congress had passed the Act almost unanimously and the President had signed it into law. From a congressional standpoint this seemed to exemplify Executive Branch disregard for legislative mandates. Whether or not the creation of the Office of Environmental Education was palatable to it, a representative of the Administration had no legal basis for implying that the bureaucracy would follow the will of Congress if it saw fit. This was the first in a series of official pronouncements that led proponents of the Act to distrust the intentions of HEW officials to carry out the purposes of the Act once it had been passed.

Byrd felt that more information was necessary about the implementation plans, and he asked Cardwell to provide a statement for the hearing record of "what steps were being taken to initiate the program in fiscal year 1971 and how far you (the Executive Branch) intend to go in that direction."

Byrd's role at this juncture in the history of the Act was brief but very important. Normally, appropriations requests for the Office of Education are handled by the Subcommittee on Labor and Health, Education and Welfare Appropriations in both the Senate and the House. The Senate supplemental bill included a plethora of requests for budgetary increases totaling over $2 billion. Obviously, Byrd could not make decisions on all of these requests without the benefit of advice from members and professional employees of the appropriations subcommittees having jurisdiction over these various areas. In this case Harley M. Dirks, a key staff aide for the Senate Labor and HEW Appropriations Subcommittee, was present at the hearings to assist the Byrd subcommittee on Office of Education and other HEW matters. This was his area of expertise, and this was the function he normally provided during the consideration of supplemental appropriations. His presence helped to ensure that there would be coordination between ad hoc requests and the upcoming budget cycle for FY 1972. The coordination was a matter of briefing, conferring with, and receiving instruction from Senator Warren Magnuson (D–Wash.), Chairman of the Subcommittee on Appropriations for Labor and HEW, and other key subcommittee members including the senior minority member.

The day after the hearings Cardwell sent a memo to HEW Secretary Richardson telling him what had happened the day before. He mentioned that Senator Byrd "quite unexpectedly" announced that the Senate was considering an amendment to the 1971 supplemental appropriations bill to provide $5 million for implementing the Environmental Education Act. The Comptroller said he had told Byrd that "the Commissioner of Education had organized the Office of Environmental Education" and "that a final decision had not been made as to whether we might propose separate funding for Fiscal Year 1972. [As the budget for 1972 stands now, no monies are supported for this purpose.]" *

On December 4 Nelson appeared before the subcommittee to testify in favor of his previous request. Although he had asked for the full $5 million, he indicated that he could "live with" about half that amount.

In his remarks before the subcommittee he said:

> I think $2 million at least would get the Office underway and would fund some good projects very selectively across the country.

---

* The hearing record indicates that Cardwell had not told Byrd that an Office of Environmental Education "was organized." Why he said to Richardson that he had done this is uncertain.

> SENATOR BYRD: Have you had any indication, Senator,
> that the Office of Education would welcome an
> appropriation at this time of, say, $2 million or that
> the mechanics are such that the Office of Education
> could proceed to feasibly expend something in the
> neighborhood of $2 million at this point?
> SENATOR NELSON: I am satisfied there would not be
> any problem in $2 million.

The letter from Richardson that Cardwell had promised
to Byrd was received shortly after Nelson testified, but it
was unresponsive to Byrd's question about the steps taken
to initiate the program. Richardson began:

> You requested that this Department provide you with
> additional information on our plans for funding the
> Environmental Education Act. . . .

He then discussed what the Office of Education would do
with the $2 billion in fiscal year 1971, but nowhere did he
state what plans had been, were being, or might be made
to establish a program and, very importantly, to install the
office specified in the legislation. Nowhere in his reply did
the Secretary refer to any entity that would carry out the
purposes of the bill, and thus he avoided the controversial
issue of the statutory mandate HEW had been given to
create a particular organization to administer the Act.

Richardson continued:

> We are undertaking the same type of *programming*
> for FY 1972 and will be prepared to describe in detail
> to both the Senate and the House appropriations com-
> mittees what funds will be devoted to the objectives

of the Environmental Education Act as soon as the President's budget is submitted next January. [*Italics added*]

The key word here is "programming." This procedure, in contrast to "reprogramming," would not require congressional approval for the shifting of funds from one program to another, and therefore the Executive Branch could not be held closely accountable to Congress for its actions. For this reason funding as described in the Secretary's letter could become nothing more than a paper exercise, if the Administration so desired.

At this time the problems of getting the appropriation through Congress before adjournment were compounded by an impending threat of six possible filibusters, which are only possible in the Senate. In the hectic pace common at the end of a Congress (in this case, the Ninety-first), a tactic often used to enact or stop the passage of a highly controversial bill is to threaten to hold a prolonged debate on it or another measure, which can prevent all other legislation from being acted upon. A filibuster can be stopped only with a two-thirds vote against it. This is called invoking cloture.

The six issues on which the Senate might debate at length were: a provision to prohibit the President from sending American ground troops or advisors into Cambodia; federal subsidization of the Supersonic Transport (SST); the question of providing low-interest loans to Latin-American and Asian countries; the issue of credit sales of American military arms in particular to Israel; and two potentially explosive amendments attached to a popular Social Security bill, one calling for a stiffening of welfare reform and the other for harsher trade quotas.

With so many potential obstacles to the passage of any legislation, the President sternly warned Congress that if a logjam developed he would call the Congress back into special session immediately after the first of the year. As it happened, only the SST issue was subjected to a delaying debate, which set the stage for killing the program in March of the following year.

Meanwhile, the supplemental requests regarding HEW had to be discussed with Senator Magnuson before Byrd made any decisions. Magnuson gave his approval to the funds requested for the Environmental Education Act, thus giving Byrd a strong bargaining position when the supplemental appropriations bill went to conference.

Regarding the House side, Senator Nelson phoned Representative Daniel Flood (D–Pa.), Chairman of the House Subcommittee on Labor and HEW Appropriations, and asked him to consider approving the $2 million during the House/Senate conference to be held to iron out the differences between this bill and the previously passed House version. Flood was the key man on the House side, and getting his assent would almost certainly guarantee that the appropriation would stay in the bill during the conference session. Nelson felt there was a special urgency in talking with the House Chairman because he had learned that the Executive Branch was trying to persuade Flood to block the environmental education appropriation request. The conversation was short; the Senator pointed out the virtues of the legislation and the rationale for the $2-million request, but Flood did not commit himself and said he would see what could be done. Since the Environmental Education Act was passed after the House had held supplemental-appropriations hearings, the Chairman would tend to prefer waiting until the next fiscal year's budget was presented in January.

The bill, which contained a $2-million appropriation for the Act, was reported out of the Senate Appropriations Committee on December 11 and was passed by the Senate on December 14. Despite the difficulties of timing on the House side, the House conferees agreed to the Senate funding amendment for environmental education, and the bill containing the funding request was reported out of conference on December 15. The supplemental-appropriations legislation was approved by Congress on December 22. The Executive Branch was confronted with another eleventh-hour finish, and it would now be hard-pressed not to ask for an appropriation for FY 1972.

THE SECOND ROUND: THE HOUSE

The congressional action in late December had a positive effect for the bill on the Administration's budget for FY 1972. It was apparent from the HEW Comptroller's testimony, his subsequent memorandum to Richardson, and the Secretary's reply to Senator Byrd that the Executive Branch had serious reservations about requesting a formal appropriation for FY 1972. However, congressional action for FY 1971 had made it difficult for the Administration to ignore this congressional funding mandate, and a $2-million request was included in the President's budget request for FY 1972.

The House appropriations subcommittee began hearings on the Office of Education's FY 1972 budget in February, giving environmental education brief and spotty attention. Chairman Flood was concerned about the size of the amount that was to come out of the $2-million request for administrative and Advisory Council expenses. He thought the figure was exceedingly high for such a small budget. Flood replied to an Administration witness who defended this allocation that, "You are going to get nearly $400,000 to administer a $2-million fund. That is what happened to the Penn Central Railroad." Later in the hearings Representative Garner E. Shriver (R–Kan.) asked Commissioner of Education Marland if an Advisory Council had been created. Marland answered:

> We have an Advisory Council now being formed with some of the outstanding ecologists in the country as a part of it. Their papers are now in motion and invitations are going out this week.

However, the formation of the Advisory Council was not officially announced for another six months.

This lack of substantial interest in the Environmental Education Act on the part of the Flood subcommittee was to be expected because the subcommittee was dealing with a budget request totaling tens of billions of dollars. A subcommittee responsible for analysis and review of all the HEW and Labor Department programs would find the $2-million environmental-education program minuscule.

The proponents of the bill considered the Environmental Education Act of much greater importance and higher priority than a $2-million appropriation would indicate. Therefore, Nelson sent a letter to Flood on March 5 asking for the full funding authorized in the legislation—$15 million. Flood indicated his support of Nelson's objective but thought it would not be possible for his subcommittee and the full committee members to vote in favor of any increase in the president's budget for environmental education.

THE SECOND ROUND: THE SENATE

The Senate appropriations hearings on the Office of Education began in May, well after those on the House side were finished, and the Environmental Education Act was discussed on May 18. Questions about the status of the required office were raised but not directly answered.

> SENATOR MAGNUSON: The Environmental Education Act calls specifically for the creation of an Office of Environmental Education within the Office of the Commissioner. What is the current status of your plans to establish an Office of Environmental Education as called for by the Act?
>
> DR. DAVIES [Office of Education Deputy Associate Commissioner for Development]: Shortly after Commissioner Marland took over, we established a separate unit for environmental education within the new Office of Priority Management in the Office of the Commissioner. This unit is responsible for administering a coordinated environmental education effort within the Office of Education, including implementation of the $2 million program authorized specifically under the Environmental Education Act.

SENATOR MAGNUSON: What arrangements have been
made for an Office of Environmental Education to
coordinate funds from other Office of Education
programs in environmntal education programs as
defined by the Act?

DR. DAVIES: This is being performed by the special
environmental education unit established within
our Office of Priority Management.

When asked about the existence of an office, Dr. Davies
referred to an "environmental education" unit," leaving its
official status unclear.

Upon the request of the chairman, Davies provided for
the record a breakdown of the $13 million in funds from
other program authorities that the Administration would
commit to environmental education projects, in addition
to the money requested under the authority of the Act.
This would have brought the total funds targeted for environmental education up to $15 million, which would
equal the total authorization for FY 1972. This was the
figure former Commissioner Allen had stated before Congress that the Office of Education would expend in that
fiscal year.

Congress had no guarantee that the $13 million would
be redirected by the Office of Education to support projects actually coming under the concept of environmental
education as defined in the Act. If OE identified only
major programs which were supporting environmental
education, it would be nearly impossible for Congress to
determine how applicable the specific activities were. But
if Congress were given a project-by-project breakdown
and a brief description of each project, it would be easier
to discern whether or not the Office of Education was

doing what it said it would do. Because most of the grants are awarded at the end of the fiscal year, the bulk of this information could not be made available until that time.

On May 24 Nelson sent a letter to Magnuson requesting that Congress appropriate the entire $15 million authorized in the Act. Nelson knew that the environmental education staff had received almost 2,000 proposals requesting a total of about $75 million, and that all of these had to compete for the $2 million appropriated for FY 1971. In his letter Nelson pointed out that it would be possible "to utilize even more than the $15 million authorized by the Act." Senators Mondale (D–Minn.) and Mansfield (D–Mont.) also sent letters to the Chairman expressing their strong support for the purposes of the Act and their hope that it would receive greatly increased funding.

These recommendations were taken into consideration during the following markup sessions of the House and Senate Appropriations committees. On April 7, 1971, the House passed the Office of Education appropriations bill, leaving untouched the $2 million for environmental education that the Administration had requested. On June 10 the Senate passed its version of the appropriations bill with $5 million included for the Act. The requests of Nelson and others and the interest of the Senate Appropriations Subcommittee Chairman had resulted in the incorporation into the Senate bill of a $3-million increase over the requested funding level. The House/Senate conferees comprised on a $3.5-million appropriation for FY 1972.

The increase in funds for the Environmental Education Act was the result of a congressional effort, as was the bill's first funding. Congress was maintaining its pressure, but there is only so much that can be accomplished in the appropriations process, because the main supporters of the Act were not members of the Appropriations committees, and they could exert only limited influence on these highly powerful bodies.

7

The Operational Phase

THE MAVERICK ORGANIZATION

THE ENVIRONMENTAL Education Act was administered by a maverick organization in the Office of Education that operated mainly outside the bureaucracy. It consisted of a handful of OE empolyees and students who attempted to bypass the organizational machinery wherever possible because they felt that the machinery generally could not respond quickly or effectively to new ideas, regardless of what was intended at the policy-making level. The continued efforts of the staff complemented the legislative activities.

Two employees of OE's Institute for International Studies were given permission to work on environmental education during the summer of 1969. The staff they formed, which officially came into existence on February 9, 1970, with the Commissioner's creation of the Environ-

mental Education Task Force, survived several redesig-
nations and five physical moves to become the core group
for the newly legislated program. It was usually at the
level of four permanent OE employees and three students.
For most of the staff's existence, until it had a permanent
director in May 1971, it functioned as an underground
organization operating in bureaucratic limbo. Its lack of
official status prevented it from establishing the mechanism that it, too, would need to ensure the continued
existence of its program, but this informality also allowed
the staff an operational freedom that enabled it to establish and fund a grant program for a totally new educational concept in a fraction of the usual time.

The Environmental Education Studies Staff continued
on after April, 1970, when the task force it had been
created to coordinate and support was allowed to expire
after completing its report. Technically, the assignment, or
detail, of the staff members expired also, but they continued to function as before, reporting and responsible to
no one. The task force director stayed on in his position as
Special Assistant to the Commissioner until the following
October, and helped run interference for the program.

From this point until the bill was passed in October the
staff concentrated on defining the state of the art in environmental education and identifying environmental
programs mainly in the Office of Education that might be
funded under legislation already existing. They worked
with and against a competitive OE planning group set up
within the Bureau of Research to develop between May
and August a five-year projection for the new program.
Each program unit in OE had to prepare a report on what
it was doing that could be considered environmental edu-

cation and what it could do in the future. The OE effort resulted in an elaborate and tremendously expensive projection that would have affected almost every program in OE, but the plan was never used.

During the summer of 1970 student interns assisted in coordinating a countrywide survey to identify existing programs and federal and nonfederal legislation related to environmental education. A consultant produced four booklets of articles on environmental education, and the staff itself prepared a general philosophical booklet entitled "Education That Cannot Wait."

The EE Staff was able to identify and help get funds allocated for other purposes during this period, with varying degrees of success in terms of program goals. One of the most promising was a proposal for a broad environmental-type television program that would be co-sponsored by the Corporation for Public Broadcasting. It would be called the Public Broadcasting Environmental Center (PBEC), and its approach would be similar to the Corporation's "Sesame Street" project of which Allen was very fond. When the PBEC idea was presented to the Commissioner, he liked the concept and decided to give it strong support. After extensive negotiating and proposal rewriting, and with the aid of direct White House intervention, he was finally able to provide a $600,000 planning grant from OE's Bureau of Cooperative Research, but the program never got beyond the planning stage, and the grant was not renewed.

The largest project in which the EE Staff was involved was the establishment of a program to train environmental technicians, taking advantage of unused Department of Labor funds. The money was provided for the

JOBS program under the Manpower Development Training Act, which was supposed to be spent with the concurrence of HEW. If the money was not spent, it would revert to the Treasury. HEW saw this as an opportunity to exercise power it had previously disregarded. The EE Staff was tipped off that the money was available and, with the aid of two consultants, they hammered out an agreement between HEW and the Department of Labor that HEW would spend some of the money training technicians to work in existing environmental jobs. HEW won a $15-million package; $8 million was used for training in health fields, and about $7 million went to train environmental technicians.

During May and early June Commissioner Allen provided another $200,000 from money that could be spent at his discretion to fund four additional programs, chosen from proposals relating to the environment that had been received in the Office of Education. This number of early requests was evidence of the grass-roots nature of the environmental education movement, as well as a response to the Commissioner's speech and to the publicity produced by the congressional activity.

A problem all this activity created for the bureaucracy was that the EE Studies Staff was supposed to be a planning unit, as its name indicated, rather than a new functional office. The task-force report and the planning document produced by the Bureau of Research were supposed to indicate what each of the units in OE would do, and the bureau chiefs were to report on their progress at each of the Commissioner's monthly management meetings. It didn't work out that way. The maverick EE staff was becoming operational, although the Commissioner had not intended that this would happen. Altogether, they spent some $8 million on environmental education projects during fiscal year 1970, including the $7 million from the Manpower funds.

Meanwhile, Allen was coming to the end of his year as head of the Office of Education. He had not been able to persuade the many individual units under his command to conduct as many EE programs as he wished. He was fired in June 1970, but his position was not filled until the end of the year.

The appointment of the new Commissioner, Sidney Marland, came one month after the Environmental Education Act had been signed into law in October 1970. The EE effort in the Office of Education had been one of Allen's priority areas, but with his departure from the federal government its existence became precarious. At that time there could be no assurance that a new Commissioner would allow it to continue. From this viewpoint the legislation was passed at a perfect time, in that it gave environmental education a statutory base and mandated that it would become a permanent feature of OE. The legislation removed it from the whim of succeeding Commissioners or at least did so over the three years for which funds were authorized.

Shortly after the new Commissioner took office, and following the first oversight hearings, the unit was officially designated as simply "Environmental Education" with no indication of whether it was a staff, an office, or a program. In December it was brought under the newly created Office of Priority Management, along with other programs that OE considered of high priority, such as Model Cities, Right-to-Read, and Drug-Abuse Education, programs that were also broad in scope and affected many program authorities. While the new unit's status was not yet defined organizationally, its position was now much more secure. The next step was for the staff to begin preparing to carry out the Act.

CATOCTIN

Even before the bill was enacted into law, the EE Staff was looking for a means of making other government agencies aware of environmental education. The staff wanted to develop an information network (with OE at the center and in a leadership role) and to establish an "underground" of contacts within the federal bureaucracy. The usual procedure would be for an agency to recommend the creation of some form of interagency coordinating mechanism, but the staff did not favor this route because they wanted to reach specific individuals who would be truly interested in environmental education and who could initiate activities within their own agencies.

The staff devised a plan to hold a series of informal conferences designed to skirt the usual requirements for organization and accountability. Together with employees of the National Park Service and the Environmental Protection Agency, they scheduled the conferences at a former Job Corps Training Center maintained by the National Park Service in the Catoctin Mountains of Maryland. Eventually, some 50 agencies or subagencies of the federal government were involved, including the Peace Corps, the Department of Housing and Urban Development, the Department of the Interior, NASA, the Department of Agriculture, and other offices in OE. A number of private citizens also participated.

There was no official sponsor and no budget. The National Park Service provided the training site, and each participant paid $15 or $20 for living expenses. The government employees were on travel orders from their own agencies, and they often pooled their travel money to pay for bringing in outsiders, including students who were involved in an exemplary environmental education program to demonstrate some of the techniques they were employing. The procedure was unorthodox but not illegal. Although nothing was said to the Commissioner's office about the conferences, some people at the policy level in OE knew what was going on and saw no reason to interfere.

In all, nine interagency conferences were held from December 1970 to September 1971. Most took place in the first three months of 1971, before the staff plunged into the huge task of preparing to fund grant proposals.

The Catoctin center was close enough to Washington to be easily reached by automobile, but far enough away that the participants would have to stay overnight and leave their other responsibilities behind. The conferences ordinarily began Tuesday afternoon and ended at noon on Thursday. The typical format would be to open with a general discussion on environmental education during the first evening to get the participants into the spirit of what would follow. Following another discussion the next morning, they would be divided into groups and assigned a specific problem such as drafting a project proposal or formulating a definition of environmental education. At the end of the conference they would reassemble and present their group reports.

Three special-interest conferences were also conducted for teachers, congressional staffers, and theologians. In the

Hill conference the instructors were students who demonstrated a way of tackling environmental problems. The staffers chartered a bus for Catoctin, and on the way they made five stops at different points along the Potomac River to take samples of the water. When they arrived, they analyzed the samples, noting the differences between the water at downtown Washington and that from further upstream. During the rest of the session they discussed the particular problem of water pollution, including all the technical and nontechnical factors involved in what must be done to clean up the water. In the conference on ethics the theologians explored the possible relationships between the Judeo-Christian tradition and the environmental crisis, discussing man's role as one of stewardship rather than one of dominance over nature.

The lack of formal sponsorship led to an odd problem of protocol when the First Lady, Mrs. Nixon, was invited to attend one of the water-testing conferences. She was expected to be at the nearby Presidential retreat at Camp David, but as it turned out she was going to Key Biscayne, Florida, and her secretary had to identify the sponsor so she could decline the invitation. This was not easy, since there was no official sponsor. The secretary received the invitation note on Monday and on Tuesday asked the Environmental Protection Agency (EPA) who was in charge of the conference. The EPA referred her to the National Park Service, which in turn referred her further, and it was Thursday, the day this particular conference was to begin, before she had singled out the Environmental Education Staff. That happened only because the head of the staff's parent Office of Priority Management overheard discussions of the White House inquiry at OE and quickly notified the staff to return the call. The only person in the office was a Peace Corps employee on loan, who finally called the White House and made arrangements for Mrs. Nixon's personal note to be picked up.

Throughout its history the environmental education program operated in an ad hoc style, of which the Catoctin conferences were a prime example. At Catoctin the staff attempted to communicate laterally rather than vertically. The administrative procedure for such conferences should have passed up the Office of Education's chain of command at least to the Commissioner's office, or even to the office of the Secretary of HEW, reaching across agency lines at that level and filtering back down through the other agencies.

The Catoctin conferences were immensely successful, and the results began to appear in the other agencies. The National Science Foundation sponsored a national conference on environmental education curricula, and the Environmental Protection Agency, the Department of the Interior, and the U.S. Forest Service established task forces on environmental education.

THE FUNDS ARE RELEASED

The President's signing of the supplemental-appropriations bill on January 8, 1971, providing $2 million for the Environmental Education Act, was the EE Staff's official sanction to set in motion the complicated process of accepting, evaluating, and selecting project proposals. At about the same time the staff learned through their contacts that $2 million would be included in the federal budget for FY 1972 specifically for EE. The program now had some promise of tenure. It would be difficult for the money to be reprogrammed or the program to be moved elsewhere in the HEW organization because Congress would have to give its approval. The task at this point was to establish a mechanism for getting the FY 1971 funds obligated by June 30, the end of the fiscal year.

There was one more obstacle between the completed congressional appropriation and the actual release of the funds to the specific office in which they would be spent. Before the money could be used, it had to be apportioned to the agency by the Office of Management and Budget. The procedure is for the agency to send to OMB a document called an apportionment schedule. OMB signs the document and sends it, in this case, to the HEW budget office. HEW then issues a release document to the budget office within the Office of Education, and the unit responsible for the program is notified that the money is available. Normally, apportionment is an automatic procedure, that is usually completed in about a month. For the Environmental Education Act it took more than two months. Technically, at this point the President had the power to impound the money, that is, to order OMB not to release the funds. However, this is a rare occurrence that is usually used only when Congress appropriates substantially more funds for a program than the Administration requested, or when the President is adamantly opposed to a program. Although OMB felt the EE program was inconsistent with the Administration's philosophy, it did not consider it worth the effort to halt it. If OMB wanted to kill the program, there is no evidence that it attempted to do so.

The final step was for the HEW budget office to issue a release document to the Office of Education indicating that the funds had been apportioned in OMB. From here on in, the money must be spent for the purpose intended. The problem was one of time. When the release document was transmitted to OE, less than four months remained until the end of the fiscal year, and FY 1971 money had to be obligated on paper by the budget office no later than June 30. This meant that the entire funding cycle would have to be completed by that time. The intent of Congress would have to be translated into a statement of priorities and a set of guidelines on submitting program proposals. The guidelines would have to be distributed to those requesting grants, and all the proposals received would have to be evaluated; those selected would be given grants out of the money that had been appropriated. Actually, the staff had been preparing for this process since the beginning of the year on the assumption that the appropriation would come through, and they were already at work on the priorities and guidelines.

The process could be completed, but the odds were not all that good. Even before the funds were released, the EE Staff had received some 300 unsolicited project proposals, the final total was almost 2,000. This was twice as many proposals as most well-established OE programs receive during a full year of operation. If the staff could not follow through with the funding cycle before the end of June, the program's money would have been returned to the Treasury. None of the projects would have received funding for that year, although money had already been requested by the Administration for the next fiscal year.

THE GUIDELINES

Guidelines are the agency's official interpretation of the intent of Congress as it is expressed in the hearings, the committee reports, the speeches, and all the other documentation that is produced over the bill's legislative history. They provide the information and instructions for submitting project proposals. Once the guidelines are drafted, they must be passed to the agency's general counsel for approval, and then an official version is published in *The Federal Register*.

Based upon its interpretation of the legislation, OE set a high priority on getting the local communities involved in the education process to demonstrate that education should not be left to education institutions alone. This approach is atypical of program operation in the other authorities of OE. The staff wanted to work through community centers and private citizens' groups to encourage interactions among all elements of the community. They had a limited program with meager resources, and they intended to get as much community involvement in environmental education as they could for their money. They feared that if such relatively tiny amounts as they would have were distributed totally in the education establishment they would be immediately absorbed and disappear. Brademas, however, whose national constituency was in the education establishment, felt that it should have a more prominent role in environmental education.

The staff kept the guidelines broad and open-ended, partially due to the time factor, partially due to their limited knowledge of what they wanted, and partially due to the nature of the legislation itself. Problems arose in the categorization of programs. The law was really about an educational process as well as a subject, and many of the proposals might fall into several of the categories specified in the bill, such as teacher training and curriculum development, or be perfectly suited to none.

After the guidelines were completed they were submitted to the HEW General Counsel for approval. Then they were printed in a handbook, and 10,000 copies were distributed on April 15. The deadline for submitting proposals was set at May 26, a scant month and a half later. Roughly 500 institutions had already been in touch with the EE office, so some of the requesters knew what to expect. The majority did not.

THE PROPOSALS: EVALUATION AND SELECTION

The response was overwhelming. While the staff had planned for a maximum of 1,200 requests, almost 2,000 were received. The result was pandemonium in the EE office. The staff located some additional, temporarily unoccupied offices. Without permission, they moved in and scrounged chairs and desks where they could. They augmented the planned readers by bringing in a number of "street people," almost all of whom had been employed at one time or other by the environmental-action groups. Proposals were stacked in piles on the office floors, with staff, student interns, consultants, and street people bumping into each other, telephones ringing, a prevalence of long hair and blue jeans, and the pervasive sounds of hard rock. Commissioner Marland had never seen anything quite like it, but on the whole he was sympathetic.

In order to get all 1,925 proposals read and evaluated the staff devised a review process designed to be as objective as possible and to draw on a wide range of expertise. As required by OE practice every request had to be read by at least two outside readers; the final review and selection would be conducted by the staff. Specialists in environmental fields were invited to read proposals, with the largest percentage from the federal government. Others were specialists, university faculty members, and representatives of urban-planning groups and private environmental groups and foundations. Most were unpaid volunteers.

The first step of the evaluation process for the staff was to give each proposal a preliminary scanning to make sure it met the technical requirements specified in the Handbook. This was almost an around-the-clock task in itself, with the staff working to keep ahead of the readers. The proposals were logged in, checked, and filed in appropriate categories.

The second step was the evaluation process. Each proposal that passed the preliminary screening was read by two or more specialists, neither of whom saw the other's evaluation. On every proposal the reader completed two evaluation sheets based on the guidelines. If one reader gave a proposal a high rating and another a low-rating, it was read by a third specialist. The scores were tabulated and the top 400 chosen for further evaluation.

The third phase, evaluation by the environmental-education staff, took place at a private inn in Harper's Ferry, Virginia, where the staff retreated for a week from the chaos in Washington to debate the merits of the programs they had already read. The 400 proposals were reviewed and cut to 150, and, after another review, to 90. Geographical distribution and nonduplication of existing programs were factored in.

It was at this point that the effects of political pressures to fund specific projects entered into the decision making. The process works in two directions: someone goes to his congressman to request help on a project; the congressman's office approaches the agency, they may receive favorable treatment, depending upon who the congressman is. Conversely, the agency may try to encourage the interest of key congressmen in projects in their districts to strengthen the program's constituency. A desirable result of this political game is to seek out important allies on the Hill, such as appropriations committee members, and to engage them in a productive quid pro quo.

The Office of Environmental Education cut the number of proposals to 74, and toward the end of June the list was forwarded to the Commissioner of Education for approval of the awards. Of the nearly 2,000 proposals fewer than 4 percent were chosen.

THE PROJECTS

Of the $2 million appropriated for the first year of the Environmental Education Act, $1.75 million was available for grants, after the program's operating expenses were deducted. This relatively small amount of money was awarded in 74 grants, parceled out through 31 states and the District of Columbia. Among these 74 were the first available under federal education legislation for community education that would not be conducted through a university and for the training of noneducators.

The activities that could be supported were divided into two general priority groups, and the applicants naturally tended to go for the higher priorities. Priority Group I consisted of community environmental education projects, special activities for state planning groups, environmental education centers, noneducational-personnel development, and comprehensive community-education models. Forty-seven of the 74 projects funded, or about two-thirds were from this group. Priority Group II included curriculum development, dissemination, educational-personnel training, and elementary and secondary-education programs, among other categories. Awards ranged from $1,600 for a local conservation commission to $71,000 for an urban school district.

The proposals were considered in three general categories: small grants, large grants, and statewide plans. The first was the "mini-grant" section defined in Section V of the legislation, and discussed in Chapter 3. Grants in this section were for amounts of $10,000 or less, their purpose being specifically to reach nonprofit organizations with small staffs, including volunteer groups, citizens' groups, and other public and private nonprofit organizations working in the environmental field. The Act specified that the grants be used for courses, workshops, seminars, institutes, symposiums, and conferences. The only proviso for citizens' groups and volunteer organizations was that they had been in existence one year prior to applying for a grant.

Of the 74 funded projects 17 actually qualified in the small-grant category. The largest number of grants and the greatest amount of money went to private organizations. About 1,000 proposals were received in this category, indicating the substantial interest in the program outside the education community.

In the large-grant category 900 proposals were received, and the highest number of grants were awarded in the areas of community environmental education projects, curriculum development, and environmental education centers. The highest number of grants in this category went to colleges and universities, followed by local and state education agencies, but almost all of the college programs funded were for activities to be conducted outside the college itself.

The third category was statewide plans, or, in the jargon of the guidelines, "statewide evaluation and dissemination" projects. This distinction was made at the OE General Counsel's suggestion so that statewide planning activities per se could be funded. Since a large amount of planning may be evaluation, statewide planning groups could accomplish their planning objectives under this section. Eighteen proposals were received for statewide plans from a wide variety of sponsoring agencies, and five were funded.

In all three categories there were some successes, some mediocre performances, and a few disasters. But this was a totally new and experimental program, and a certain degree of risk was involved in the first years of operation. There was disagreement as to where the program should go or what it should do, and differences of opinion existed within both branches of government as to what environmental education actually was.

The Small Grants

The amounts of money distributed as "small grants" were infinitesimal by federal standards. One of the most dollar-effective was a program conducted by the Illinois Federation of Women's Clubs. With a grant of $1,800 the Illinois women developed an educational program about the Little Calumet Watershed for students, community residents, and industry. The women spent the summer gathering information from government agencies and local pollution boards, and during the fall and winter they gave presentations to schools and clubs on problems they had identified. Later in the year, after extensive research and consultation, they began discussing environmental problems with local industries.

They arranged for the schools to sponsor contests about problems pertaining to the watershed, with savings bonds as prizes. For kindergarten through third-grade children, they designed a watershed coloring book, and for small groups of Scouts and junior high students they prepared a "watershed walk." For third through sixth grades there was a poster contest; for seventh and eighth there was an essay competition on suggested solutions to environmental problems and a mystery-story contest on the theme, "Who killed the watershed?" with the basic facts and clues provided. Other activities included litter hikes and talks and lectures in the schools.

For adults there were lectures and meetings with clubs and church groups; a home-ecology handbook was prepared for housewives; a weekly ecological "Dear Abby" column was written for local newspapers; attendance at public hearings and the watchdogging of local construction activity were organized; environmental displays were erected in local supermarkets.

In their research and inventory phase, in preparation for confronting the industries, the women collected films and environmental literature on water quality and flood control. They organized study groups to inventory various problem areas and to make reports on sewer systems, sanitary districts, city ordinances, pollution sources, landfills, district and village policy, etc.

The program was run on a shoestring, like the federal

environmental education program itself, and it depended upon the very active participation of some 24 women in a broad range of community activities.

Among other projects funded as "small grants" was an attempt to broaden the educational potential of the ENACT Ecology Center, an organic gardening project in Ann Arbor, Michigan, established by the University of Michigan, which received $9,700 to conduct tours, teacher workshops, and field courses for area schools on organic gardening and ecological principles. Sample topics were pest control using natural predators, soil-moisture control through plant spacing and mulching, and general maintainance of the soil ecosystem. Additional small-grant projects included programs to train minority-group community leaders in California on environmental issues, to produce video environmental tapes for the Hawaiian closed-circuit instructional television system, and to establish a resource center for expressing environmental grievances and seeking relief for the inhabitants of a low-income housing project in Boston.

Many of the grants were highly experimental. The staff did not know exactly what kinds of programs would be most productive, and in some cases they learned more than they expected to learn. One proposal in California was to hire an environmental administrator and to publish a bilingual newspaper for Mexican-American migrant workers, with the purpose of disseminating environmental and health information. When the project was visited later in the year, an OE staffer found that other money had been used to print the newspaper while the workers looked for a physician they could hire for the $10,000. They considered the doctor of higher priority than an environmental worker.

The biggest fiasco of the first year's operation of the Environmental Education Act was a proposal from a group in Oakland, California, to operate an environmental-training program in a 10-block ghetto area in Oakland. The proposal was a sketchy one, at best; it was to train six youths in "landscape maintenance" as a possible career, while demonstrating to the community residents how they could improve their surroundings. The program was funded for $10,000. During the course of the year an evaluator visited the project and found that the address given in submitting the proposal was a loan agency. He was informed that the organization no longer existed. It, the project, and the director were nowhere to be found; a letter addressed to the director was returned, stamped "addressee unknown."

On the whole, however, the mini-grants were a successful experiment. Plans were being made for their replication in other HEW programs during the second year of funding, and they were stressed in the environmental-education program.

The Large Grants

Two contrasting large-grant programs were a community-education project in California conducted by the Portola Wilderness School in Menlo Park, funded for $37,000, and a curriculum-development project carried out by the Atlanta public-schools system on a $71,000 grant. In the first a team method was tried, and in the second an individual study process.

The wilderness program was a yearlong project involving 20 students from a lower-income high school in an attempt to prevent the real-estate development of San Bruno Mountain, one of the last open spaces in a San Francisco suburb. The dispute was over a proposed rezoning for development purposes. The project began in the summer with three weeks of studying basic problem-solving techniques. The study session was followed by the most significant feature of the training: a two-week backpacking trip into a national forest, with the objective of bringing the group together in sharing the physical chores of camping, with the stress on building confidence as well as group cooperation. The results of this individual discovery process were to be transmitted into an urban setting. During the next phase the students divided into teams to decide how to attack the problem. Next they disseminated their findings with the aid of videotape presentations and talks before community groups, and they devised a San Bruno Mountain puppet show for elementary-school children, who could take the message home to their parents. Their efforts, along with those of other groups, convinced the city zoning board to postpone its decision on rezoning for the time being. Another important accomplishment was that the school worked out a system for deriving traditional grades for the students, even though time had not been spent in the classroom structure. This is a requirement of state boards of education that such programs find difficult to meet. The students worked well together and were productive even though they were not all A-level students.

The Atlanta schools conducted a pilot project that was to lead to the development of a complete environmental curriculum. In two Atlanta high schools tenth, eleventh, and twelfth grade students were released from structured classes for one school quarter each in order to devote full time to studying and preparing a report on an environmental area that interested them. They could choose from the natural and man-made environments including the social milieu. During the day the students were free to travel through the city, interviewing people connected with their problems. At the end of the quarter they worked with teachers in four different areas (science, social studies, language arts, and mathematics) to develop multidisciplinary proposals. They could communicate their findings through a film, a slide lecture, or a written report. The media materials were to be used for instruction in schools and community groups. Among the topics chosen were endangered species, abortion, drugs, and one entitled "Egocentric Philosophy as a Cause of Pollution."

The response was not overwhelming, and the freedom was often abused, with no close supervision and no peer-group influence. Also, the Atlanta students did not have the background of training and confidence-building provided by Portola.

Another community-education project was carried out with a grant of $43,000 by St. Anselm's College of Manchester, New Hampshire, which focused on the watershed for the city of Manchester, an 1,800-acre swamp. The problem was one of increasing invasion of the watershed by man, damaging this ecologically fragile system and threatening the city's water supply.

The college proposed to involve students, high school and college teachers, and state officials in educational projects concerning the ecological danger. In the first phase of the program the students of three city high schools studied the watershed to become familiar with the processes of water testing and the ecological factors involved in the life and death of a lake. Through the school year four tasks were undertaken. First, classes on basic ecology related to the watershed were offered at one of the high schools, with students chosen on the basis of their interest and not their grade average. The second task was to hold community-action conferences in the spring for the public, with representatives from state conservation organizations, ecology clubs, colleges, and the political sphere. Videotapes, slides, and photographs developed by the students in the earlier phases were displayed. The third task was for St. Anselm's College and the Manchester public-school system to sponsor jointly an environmental education program in the high schools, with a "Curriculum Guide on Water Pollution" being produced. The fourth task was to enroll a group of superior students in an Advanced Ecological Studies Program offered by St. Anselm's College, based in the high school experience, but on a much higher plane of trends, meanings, etc.

A sample report produced by the students was a short photographic essay entitled "Blood River," which illustrated a conduit through which blood from a packing plant in Manchester flows directly into the Merrimack River. The photos of the brilliant red stream showed the web of hair, manure, and skin that formed on the rocks of the stream bed and the fat that congealed on the banks on cold days.

Some of the Environmental Education Act grants funded education programs conducted by museums and libraries. One such program was that of the Fairbanks Museum of Natural Science in St. Johnsbury, Vermont. The Fairbanks Museum had already been conducting lectures, demonstrations, and field trips for elementary and secondary students. The museum's emphasis was on reaching students in grades one through eight with an extensive educational schedule. It held classes in physics (astronomy, meteorology, physiogeography), chemistry, and biology, in the social sciences, anthropology, archaeology, economics, tax law, and legislative process, and in the responsibilities of municipal, state, and federal bodies. Students could visit the prepared nature areas surrounding the museum, and a 60-passenger bus was used to bring them in and to take them out on field trips. The museum also conducted teacher training, offering special courses in environmental education for teachers and providing its own staff to work at various universities, on a loan basis.

The Statewide Plans

Under the special category for statewide planning and cordination efforts programs were funded for New York, Texas, Massachusetts, Minnesota, and Colorado. Some were conducted by private organizations and some by official state entities, but none exclusively by a state department of education.

The Colorado project was carried out by the Center for Research and Education in Estes Park, in association with the Rocky Mountain Center of Environment and the Colorado Department of Education. With a $40,000 grant the Center established a state Master Advisory Planning Council representing formal and nonformal education groups, media, labor, industry, students, doctors, city officials, and planners. The Council formulated a plan for multidisciplinary teaching at all grade levels and established state environmental-education councils and an environmental-education study center.

The Massachusetts plan was conducted by the Massachusetts Audubon Society with a $30,000 grant. The society established a permanent, quasi-governmental planning, coordinating, and funding body in the form of a Trust for Environmental Education. The first task of the Trust was to assess priorities among the state's environmental needs.

In Minnesota a $40,000 grant was awarded to the state's Environmental Education Planning Committee to carry on a program authorized by the state legislature in 1969 for statewide elementary and secondary environmental education.

In Texas the grant went to a division in the office of the Governor that was working on a two-phase program of special evaluation and dissemination leading to the development of a comprehensive state environmental education plan, encompassing local and regional government activities, civic groups, and private organizations, as well as students.

The New York State program attempted, with a $27,000 grant, to develop a state plan and to coordinate education activities. The program was conducted by the New York Legislature's Commission on Youth Education in Conservation.

Most of the projects succeeded, and at least two were excellent. As with the small-grant and large-grant categories overall, the successes far outweighed the failures, and much could be learned for succeeding years.

Evaluation

The last step in the implementation process was to evaluate as many programs as possible. This step was crucial because these were pilot and demonstration projects, The concept was not so much to establish an operating program as to learn what could be done and to develop models that could be used widely.

The evaluation was conducted by staff members and outside consultants, and it was based on three criteria: content, replicability, and generating force. Questions were addressed to what materials the project contained that enabled the student to form his own environmental values; what in the program makes it able to be carried out elsewhere; and how would other school systems get excited enough about the project to try it?

By the end of the first fiscal year the evaluators had visited and reported on 73 of the 74 projects. Some were visited twice and some three or four times. The number of visits was unusual, but so was their goal. They were part of the continuing process of attempting to define environmental education for the federal government and the nation.

8

Oversight

ALMOST ONE year after the Environmental Education Act was passed Congress within three weeks held three sets of oversight hearings that inquired into the way the law was being carried out.

Oversight is the most elusive and most difficult to describe of the three major functions of Congress, and it is exercised in three different forms by legislation, appropriations and oversight (Government Operations) committees. Oversight was first spelled out as an area where Congressional action was needed in the Legislative Reorganization Act of 1946:

> . . . To assist the Congress in appraising the Administration of the law and in developing such amendments or related legislation as it may deem necessary, each standing committee of the Senate and the House of Representatives shall exercise continuous watch-

fulness of the Executive by the administrative agencies concerned of any law, the subject matter of which is within the jurisdiction of such committee.

This section of the Act emphasized the importance of congressional committees exercising constant surveillance over programs and activities in their areas of authority. In addition, the act created two new committees —the Government Operations committees of the House and Senate—that had no legislative authority and were given the explicit mandate of maintaining oversight over existing programs on all Executive Branch activities, including broad issues cutting across agency jurisdictions.

The goal of oversight in this sense is to achieve a maximum of economy and effectiveness in the conduct of federal programs, and the oversight function can have an important influence on the way the programs are administered. Although the Government Operations committees do not have jurisdiction over any specific programs, they can give visibility to Executive Branch problems through hearings, which can engender public debate and help to solve these problems.

With regard to the Environmental Education Act, one Government Operations subcommittee and two legislative subcommittees during October 1971 focused on the question of whether or not the Executive Branch had carried out the intentions of Congress or would do so.

The first was a Senate inquiry on October 8 into the effectiveness of advisory councils on a government-wide basis. Chaired by Senator Lee Metcalf (D–Mont.), the hearings were conducted by the Intergovernmental Relations Subcommittee of the Government Operations Committee. The yet-to-be-created Advisory Council on

Environmental Education was one of the subects investigated.

The second set of hearings, held on October 14, was devoted to a single broad issue—population control. It was based on a proposed Senate Joint Resolution that declared it a policy of the United States to stabilize its population. The hearings were chaired by Senator Alan Cranston (D–Cal.) and conducted by the Senate Subcommittee on Human Resources of the Labor and Public Welfare Committee. The Environmental Education Act came up because education on population control was one of the Act's goals, and the Chairman had been responsible for having it incorporated in the Act during the bill's passage.

The third and most decisive set of hearings was that conducted by the House subcommittee that had taken initial action on the bill. On October 28 the Select Education Subcommittee, chaired by Brademas, held anniversary hearings and exercised legislative oversight in a way that could be done only by a subcommittee with continuing jurisdiction.

There was no grand scheme involved in holding these three sets of hearings within such a short time, but the overall effect was greatly advantageous for the congressional proponents of the Act. The first two hearings were scheduled independently of each other, but the Brademas hearings were called in part because of the dramatic effect the first two had on the Office of Education, which in effect admitted that it had been slow in carrying out the intent of Congress. Brademas' staff aide was informed of the momentum that was building in the Senate, and he suggested the anniversary oversight hearings to Brademas, who was receptive because the timing was good.

The Brademas subcommittee was able to get a firm commitment from the Administration because Brademas knew what was being done and what was not being done, what the official excuses were, and where the arguments were the weakest. The results would not have been the same without all three hearings and without the Brademas hearings coming last.

The effect of approaching the Environmental Education Act from unexpected angles in a short time frame was to indicate to the Executive Branch that Congress considered environmental education a high-priority program—high enough to be fully implemented and included on a governmental organization chart.

THE METCALF HEARINGS

In the Metcalf hearings the Government Operations Committee was using its authority to examine an issue that cut across agency lines. It was asking to what extent advisory councils really advise on policy issues by bringing in ideas from outside the government, if they are just established by tradition to shield the program or agency from public scrutiny and criticism, or whether they were purely window dressing. The hearings focused on many councils advising various departments and agencies; on October 8 the attention of the Subcommittee came to the Environmental Education Act.

E. Winslow Turner, the Subcommittee's General Counsel, had made a thorough investigation of the legislation and administrative history beforehand and had found what he considered a violation of U.S. law. He had done his preparation well. He knew most of the answers before the questions were asked, and he caught the representatives of the Executive Branch unprepared.

Turner handled a good amount of the questioning on environmental education personally. It is not the usual practice for a subcommittee staffer to enter directly into the questioning process, but this is done in certain committees and it can be done only at the prerogative of the subcommittee chairman, who must be in attendance.

Testifying for the Administration was HEW's Assistant Secretary for Administration and Management, Dr. Rodney H. Brady, and Dr. Robert Gilkey, identified as the "Director of the Office of Environmental Education."

The General Counsel opened his part of the inquiry by pointing out that the Executive Branch had strongly committed itself to the concept of environmental education. He quoted both the President and the Commissioner of Education and outlined the congressional action of near unanimous passage of the Environmental Education Act, which called for creating an Office of Environmental Education and an Advisory Council. His questions were blunt:

> Now, an entire year after the Nelson–Brademas Act was passed, we have no Office of Environmental Education as intended by law and no Advisory Council on Environmental Education has been formed, and the implication can only seem to be at the moment that the Administration does not attach the priority that it has announced to the importance of environmental education or that HEW has been negligent in carrying out the will of Congress, or both.
> Now where is the Office? What is it? Where is the Council? When is it going to come into effect?

Dr. Brady answered that HEW planned to establish the Advisory Council in the near future and did not discuss the status of the Office. He said Commissioner Marland had invited twenty-one people to serve on the Council in July, and eighteen had accepted. He also said the Council would hold its first meeting within "the next six weeks." He then enumerated other accomplishments under the new program, such as developing the initial program priorities, awarding the first grants, and cooperating with other federal agencies. He said, ". . . I am personally convinced that we have this program off the ground and running at this point and that its pace would continue to accelerate."

The counsel deliberately steered clear of the program's substance, focusing instead on its organizational structure. He cited the bill's language about placing the office "under the supervision of the Commissioner" and asked Dr. Gilkey if he was, indeed, "directly under Commissioner Marland." Gilkey replied that he reported to an Associate Commissioner and, in answer to another question from Turner, said he did not head an office, but a program. The counsel then asked further questions he could already answer on his own. Dr. Gilkey had little alternative but to reply that he did not have line authority to coordinate the environmental education activities of the entire Office of Education and that he was not the head of an Office of Environmental Education, as the law stated he should be, because there wasn't any.

The dramatic questioning that followed was on the closeness of Dr. Gilkey's relation to the Commissioner. Turner asked how many times Gilkey had been in the Commissioner's office in the preceding two weeks. Gilkey answered not once because the Commissioner had been away.

TURNER (*continued*): How many in the last month?

DR. GILKEY: Not once.

TURNER: How many in the last two months?

DR. GILKEY: Not once.

TURNER: How many in the last six months?

DR. GILKEY: Once, I believe.

TURNER: Once?

Turner knew approximately how Gilkey would answer. The point of the questioning was that operating a priority program would necessitate working in a certain closeness with the head of the Office of Education. Dr. Brady responded that every program could not report directly to the Commissioner because there were so many that the Commissioner would not be able to carry out his administrative duties.

Senator Metcalf agreed with Brady in general, but he stressed the importance Congress gave this particular program. He said, "the fact that there hasn't been the consultation in this special area indicates that perhaps downtown you don't give it the high priority that we are giving it up here in Congress." This question about priority was a theme that figured in all three hearings. (See Appendix 2 for Commissioner Marland's reaction.)

A Rather Questionable Situation

The counsel raised a legal problem the Administration representatives apparently had not anticipated. He asked if it was not against the law to spend money before the organization, i.e., the council, was established that could legally advise on the spending.

As a lead-in Turner read from a section of the Environ-

mental Education law that spells out the authority of the
Advisory Council "to make recommendations . . . with
respect to the allocation of funds." Turner emphasized
the "special role" of this particular council—that it was to
advise on how the program's funds would be spent. He
pointed out that $2 million had already been allocated in
grants, with no council in existence.

Turner asked:

> Now, aren't you in a rather questionable situation
> here, proceeding with the implementation and payout
> of federal funds in this program without ever having
> initially established an advisory council as ordered
> by the Congress, without having issued any legal
> guidelines for the application?

He inquired if the Secretary of HEW knew when he
approved the grants that no policies for the grant process
had been established by an Advisory Council and that an
office mandated by Congress would have to have that
responsibility. Neither Dr. Brady nor Dr. Gilkey answered
the question.

Turner then played the trump card he had been holding. He revealed that he knew of a memorandum in which
the Office of Education's General Counsel had advised
Commissioner Marland that he was "skirting the law," as
Turner said, by "handing out the grants without having
the Advisory Council review them."

Asked if he knew anything about this, Dr. Gilkey said
he was aware of the memo but had not seen it. Turner
asked Dr. Brady to produce a copy of the memo for the
subcommittee, and he said he would. Shortly after, Marland privately told his staff he had never seen the memo,

and the Office of Education was unable to find it—meaning either that it did not exist or that it was lost, inadvertently or deliberately. Indications are that the memo did not exist.

THE CRANSTON HEARINGS

Senator Cranston, Chairman of the Subcommittee on Human Resources, had scheduled hearings on population-control education before the Metcalf hearings took place. The framework he used was a Senate resolution declaring it a policy of the United States to stabilize population growth. The issue was related to the Environmental Education Act, and this was a convenient means for Cranston to investigate its implementation and also to explore the broad issues of population control. Cranston had a special interest in the Act because of his amendment, which included population education as an objective.

By the time the population hearings were held, six days later, Cranston had been informed about the earlier hearings and had received copies of the testimony. Behind the scenes a Nelson staff aide had tipped off Cranston's staff and had prepared a list of questions based on the Metcalf testimony.

The witnesses for the Office of Education were Dr. Don Davies, OE's Deputy Commissioner for Development, and Dr. Gilkey. Cranston was inquiring specifically about how population education was being carried out through the Environmental Education Act. After a couple of inconclusive questions and answers he asked if Davies' office had adequate access to expertise on population education.

Davies replied that they did have access to Dr. Louis Hellman, HEW's Deputy Assistant Secretary on Health and Population Affairs. Hellman was present at the hearings, and in answer to questions directed to him he informed Cranston that his staff was a "zero." This was an indication that HEW did not consider population education a priority issue. There was apparently no staff in HEW, and no guidelines for such projects had been included in the environmental-education program.

Since Senator Nelson could not attend the hearings himself due to conflicting priorities, he presented a list of questions to be read by another subcommittee member, Senator Robert Packwood (R–Ore.). These followed up on the administrative questions raised in the Metcalf hearings. Packwood reiterated that the Act calls for an Office of Environmental Education to be created within the Commissioner's office and asked Davies where it was in the organizational structure.

Davies said that OE was in the process of shifting a number of "high-priority" programs from the defunct Office of Priority Management to an Office of Development. Among them would be the Right-to-Read and the Drug-Abuse Education program. This was being done the very week the hearings took place.

He said the environmental education program would formally become the Office of Environmental Education. The head of the Office, Dr. Gilkey, would report to the Director of the Office of Development, who reports directly to the Commissioner of Education. This was not exactly as the legislation stipulated, and although nothing more was said here, the point was not lost in the Brademas hearings that followed. More significantly, Davies had very clearly stated that no office, in the formal sense, yet existed. Brademas did not miss this point either.

Senator Packwood also asked briefly about the program's funding and about the earmarked funds for environmental education from other OE authorities. Packwood referred to letters he had exchanged with HEW Secretary Richardson the previous summer, in which Richardson said $11 million would be made available for environmental education, in addition to the $3.5 million appropriated by Congress for the Act. He asked if the money was being earmarked and how much would be for population education. Davies and Gilkey could not answer the question because the grants had not yet been made, but Davies promised a progress report by the end of fiscal 1972. Packwood replied that he would like to be kept "advised on the running scores," which was a way of serving notice that he and the other Congressional supporters considered this program important enough to be worth continually watching.

The momentum was building. By the time the action shifted to the House side some major questions about the program had been raised. Brademas and his staff realized this and decided to take advantage of the opportunity to pin the Office of Education down on its intentions, which also meant delving into such basic constitutional issues as the doctrines of separation of powers and checks and balances.

THE BRADEMAS HEARINGS

The most significant oversight hearings on the Environmental Education Act were those conducted by the bill's author, John Brademas, Chairman of the subcommittee responsible for the bill's passage in the House. This was a third example of exercising the oversight function, whereby a committee prepares legislation for passage through Congress and then checks on the quality of its implementation.

In this case the oversight came as "anniversary hearings," on October 28, 1971, almost exactly a year after the bill had been signed into law. This subcommittee had never held oversight hearings before except when reauthorization hearings were necessary. This situation is not unusual in Congress because of the competition for time with the many other subcommittee responsibilities. Also, the Congressional mode of operation is such that major emphasis is placed on new legislation, renewed or reauthorized legislation, and appropriation bills and not oversight, per se.

The results of the previous two sets of hearings were brought to the Chairman's attention, and it appeared that hearings conducted by his subcommittee would be necessary to get a definite commitment from the Office of Education that the Act would be carried out according to the law.

Commissioner Marland believed he was on uncertain ground. Just prior to the hearings he held a meeting with his lieutenants and let them know how furious he was at them for letting things develop as they did during the first two sets of hearings. He had every reason to expect that Brademas would hold him fully accountable for the issues brought out during these hearings.

In his opening statement at the hearings Brademas stressed the importance of oversight in its larger sense. He said that many subcommittees and committees, including his, have not done an adequate job in this area.

We write laws and then seemingly turn our backs on implementation, and one hopes that this subcommittee in particular will give far greater attention than we have in the past, to assure that the intent of Congress has been followed by those charged with the administering of the laws that have been passed.

Brademas noted that this was "not the first time" the committee members and the House and Senate had been concerned about the way the law had been implemented. He and his staff had been following its progress closely. He continued:

It may well be that given the nature of our constitutional system, the separation of powers, that some will not understand the skepticism that at times members of the Legislative Branch of government bring to their judgments on the way in which the Executive Branch of government, no matter which party has control of it, do carry out the laws, but in studying the Environmental Education Act, one can understand why members of Congress get irritated, for although the Act was signed into law as I said almost a year ago, no Office of Environmental Education has as yet been created or established as the law requires, no Advisory Council on Environmental Education has as yet been formed, as the law mandated.

With characteristic candor and bluntness Brademas said further:

One wonders about respect for law and order and
obeying the law, and it is quite clear at least to the
Chairman that the Administration has not obeyed the
law.

The main purpose of the hearings was to confront the
Administration, and therefore the most important witness
was the Commissioner of Education Marland. In fact, only
three other people testified: former Secretary of the Interior Stewart Udall; Nathaniel P. Reed, Assistant Secretary of the Interior for Fish, Wildlife and Parks; and Miss
Kristin Bergfeld, education director of Environmental
Action Coalition, Inc., which was one of the environmental education grant recipients.

With his tremendous prestige in the environmental field,
Udall was called on to testify first in a bit of deliberate
stage setting for the confrontation with Marland that
would follow. It was obvious that Udall would come out
strongly in favor of the bill, and he did. He said it was his
impression that the young people of the country were
ready for it, and that "the music is good, but the footwork
is slow" in getting environmental education implemented.

Executive Branch

The real substance of the hearings was in the dramatic
dialogue between Brademas and Commissioner Marland.
Brademas had the information he needed to bear down on
some of the points raised in earlier testimony, and he and
the other subcommittee members intended to take advantage of the momentum developed by the previous hear-

ings to force the Administration to declare that it would establish the office and appoint the Advisory Council.

Asked by Representative Scheuer (D–N.Y.) if there was now an Advisory Council, Marland made the surprising announcement that, indeed, there was a list of names of those who had consented to serve on it, and he would be glad to submit the list for the record.

Brademas, somewhat surprised, said he assumed the reading of the list represented the official announcement: "I followed this rather tenaciously, Mr. Commissioner, and we have had a hard time getting that announcement." He was assured that the announcement was official. Brademas asked why the appointment had taken so long, and Marland said the Office had waited three months for one "very distinguished woman" to make up her mind about serving on the Council. The Congressman replied, "Surely you are not going to try to tell a Committee of the Congress you hold up a legislative mandated Advisory Council because one person has not made up his or her mind." Marland answered, "We have made up the Council."

Actually, even at that point the list had not been fully cleared with the necessary Administration circles nor unofficially with the Senate. Although the Senate does not advise and consent in such appointments, it is traditional to clear a list of this type with the party's senior member in the Senate Labor and Public Welfare Committee.

After the list of appointees had been read, Brademas commented, "I must say, not to be overly difficult this morning, if the setting of these hearings served no other purpose than to stimulate a public announcement of this Council, that in itself is gratifying."

The selection of an Advisory Council, which in this case

had been under way since the previous January, takes place in the office of the Secretary of HEW. Names were submitted by the Office of Education, members of Congress—Nelson and Brademas, in particular—and outside sources (especially those in favor with the Republican Party). While partisanship is not officially admitted by an Administration on such seemingly bipartisan affairs, it is an important factor in the selection process. The length of time it took to assemble the Environmental Education Advisory Council was due in part to the slowness of the machinery, and the congressional sponsors felt that it indicated the Administration was giving the program a much lower degree of priority than they intended.

"Methinks Thou Doth Protest Too Much"

Marland then addressed the embarrassing question of Dr. Gilkey's access to the Commissioner, which had been raised in the Senate Government Operations Committee hearings. Marland stressed and perhaps overstressed the high priority that OE was giving to environmental education. He said:

> This is much higher in the structural order, if that is
> an important theme, than Title I, higher education,
> student aid or bilingual education.

He said further than not only is Dr. Gilkey "within access to me at an instant's notice," but he had been in Dr. Gilkey's office a number of times, and he had "spent a considerable amount of time in that office personally."

The wry answer from Brademas was, "Methinks, Mr. Commissioner, thou doth protest too much."

Marland added that when Gilkey said he had been to the Commissioner's office perhaps once in six months, he had not been asked if the Commissioner had been to his office, and at that, with laughter in the background, the subject was dropped. What Marland said was true, but it was ironic that the Commissioner would go to the Environmental Education Office and not the other way around. Things usually don't work like that in a power structure.

A central issue here was the priority with which each branch viewed the environmental-education program. As the dialogue continued Marland again and again used the term "priority" as if to give the subcommittee verbal assurance that the program was as important to the Office of Education as to Congress.

Marland explained that in the absence of an Advisory Council, OE constructed "what was for all practical purposes, . . . an ad hoc advisory committee" to weigh the 1,925 proposals that had come in. Ecologists, environmentalists, and others had worked for the Office on a part-time, day-to-day basis, Marland said, and this was consistent with the spirit of the law. The Commissioner had a good argument about what the environmental education program had accomplished, and he defended the program well. But there had been considerable slippage, and Marland had to take the blame for it.

Brademas was not satisfied. He said:

It is an old saw among politicians on the luncheon circuit about the young fellow who killed his parents, and threw himself on the mercy of the court on the grounds he was an orphan.

You really do astonish me by remarking with great passion that lacking an Advisory Council, and on a very short timetable, you were compelled to retreat to ad hoc committees.

That is your fault. That is not our fault. The law was signed a year ago.

He said that if the program has such a high priority an Advisory Council could have been appointed for it earlier. The Chairman's contention was that the Administration would never officially have created the Council and the Office had it not been for this set of oversight hearings. Though Administration officials asserted publicly and in interviews that this was in process at the time and would have eventually happened, the documented record indicates that he might have been right.

Scheuer then produced a letter dated July 13 from John Hughes, Assistant Commissioner for Priority Management, under which the program was placed at that time, which said that the selection of the Advisory Council was near completion, and the Secretary would announce the members in the near future.

"We in Congress only get elected for two years," Brademas said.

The "near future" theme appeared repeatedly. Marland had used it in February before the House appropriations hearings. Davies had used it before the second set of oversight hearings in October, two weeks earlier, saying the Office would be created in the near future. Asked for a project-by-project breakdown of the $11.2 million earmarked for environmental education from other programs for FY 1972, Davies told Brademas it could not be made available until after the projects had been chosen in the late winter or early spring; in late October this would also be the near future.

Scheuer said he hoped further formal meetings of this nature would not be required. He said the legislators preferred to have "informal meetings so that we can get on with the business of providing environmental quality education, on a more solicitous and expeditious basis than we have up to now." Dr. Marland assured Scheuer that OE shared this attitude and that the "ragged past" of the legislation was now behind them.

Dr. Marland said OE saw in the Environmental Education Act a means of getting into educational reform and renewal, and that it would provide a "catalyst—a triggering mechanism for other funding commitments within the Office of Education," as was intended by the sponsors of the bill. He listed some of the steps that had been taken to carry out the bill, and the list was substantial.

Besides taking the administrative steps already discussed, OE was supporting 74 projects at that time, Marland said, and would fund approximately 125 in the following fiscal year. Technical assistance was given to state and local organizations and to other federal agencies to develop their own environmental education activities. OE worked with the Coast Guard and Army Corps of Engineers in planning environmental-awareness training for their personnel and with the Bureau of Land Management in developing their Johnny Horizon anti-litter campaign. It also collaborated in holding training workshops and served as a clearinghouse for collecting and disseminating environmental education information of all types. In addition, he said the office was preparing several publications on environmental education.

Does the Office Exist?

Brademas then got into the debate about establishing an Office of Environmental Education. He picked up on Marland's statement earlier in the hearings that an Office of Environmental Education had been established in August.

Dr. Marland clarified that the "Office of Environmental Education" had been placed under the Office of Development in August. It had been under the Office of Priority Management, which was abolished. What Brademas was interested in was the legalities as related to the semantics.

The distinction may seem unimportant, but in government organizational charts there is a significant difference between a program, which might offhandedly be referred to as an office, and a formal administrative unit labeled a permanent Office. The existence of the less structured organization is more precarious, and its status is lower. Brademas asked again what the program was called, and Dr. Marland replied, "The Office of Environmental Education."

Brademas kept pushing on the terminology. He said:

> That is what I want to make very clear[,] that distresses me. Commissioner, you and I have had conversations privately and publicly.
> Sometimes I think we are a little hard on you up

here, and I think you an honest man, but I do not want to see this Committee deceived.

Making explicit that this was not a personal attack, he pointed out that Marland's testimony was in direct contradiction to that of Dr. Davies, who had told the Senate Subcommittee on Human Resources on October 14 that:

> This week we are in the process of changing the organization of the status of the Environmental Education Program. The Environmental Education Program will become the Office of Environmental Education.

Brademas continued:

> Now, I think any person who understands the English language and has been listening to you this morning will have the clear impression, as I had—and I am not trying to entrap you, I am trying to give you an opportunity to be honest with this Committee—that the Office of Environmental Education had been established in August.
> That is what you said. You just said, I just asked you a minute ago, you kept referring to the Office of Environmental Education.

He then said he did not know it existed and he could not see how anyone could be sure, in light of Marland's and Davies' testimony.

The Commissioner clarified his previous statement, saying that it did not exist in the formal sense. It "was a program and it remains a program to this day." He apologized for misusing the term and said it had not been his intention to mislead the Committee.

The weight of Marland's previous testimony led Brademas to conclude that the Office would never have been created as intended without Brademas' constant prodding.

What surprised the Administration was the persistance of Congress and the adroit use of the oversight function to ensure that an official commitment be clearly stated for the record.

The Commitment and the Club

Representative Ogden Reid (D–N.Y.) followed up with a specific request that the Commissioner would "raise the question of formal status with the Secretary and get a piece of paper officially establishing the office." Marland said this would be done, and in answer to Reid's further request for a commitment that the office be established in November, he said "Yes; the answer is a firm yes."

Reid also received assurances that the Office would employ seven full-time personnel. For Congress, this is reaching a long way into the administrative machinery. Such attention to administrative details is not common and is generally resented deeply by the Executive Branch, which naturally prefers to run its own house the way it sees fit. In this case the tampering was warranted, as far as the sponsors were concerned, because of what they considered blatant flouting of the legislation and because of the Administration's resistance to appropriating money for it.

Pressing further, Reid said:

> The statute here is pretty clear, that this Office will
> be under your supervision.
> May I assume that that is the case, and that you will
> accept responsibility for supervision, as appropriate
> of this Office personally, and otherwise?

Marland answered, "I accept that."

Reid also suggested that Dr. Marland and Dr. Gilkey
"may want to report to the Committee informally or in
writing, from time to time, as the program gets going,"
and Dr. Marland replied, "We would be pleased to do
that."

Brademas later warned:

> I hope that you will understand we will probably
> want to call you back in a few weeks, which is un-
> usual, I grant you, just to see how things have been
> coming along.

The threat of further hearings and possible embarrass-
ment for the Administration officials was the club Congress could use to make sure its will was felt in the
Executive Branch. The legislators made clear that they
would not hesitate to take up the club whenever they felt
necessary.

Reid's last request to Marland was for a project-by-project breakdown of the addition $11.2 million that OE had
said would be transferred from other programs. The list of
program authorities and amounts was submitted for the

record, but a project-by-project breakdown was not possible at that time.

"I think that the purport of my question must be clear," he said. "We just want to be sure that you are obeying the law."

Representative Orval Hansen (R–Idaho) had less severe words for the Administration representatives. He said, "We live in a real world where there are other priority demands on time and resources, and I can understand . . . that there are circumstances that might result in delays." Now, he said, it would be best to focus on the future, on "getting some Federal funds out to finance projects that can carry out the purposes of the legislation." He asked if the $2-million appropriation in fiscal year 1971 had all been allocated in the 74 project grants, and Marland said it had been. Hansen asked if the one-page application had been developed, as Margaret Mead suggested in the original House hearings, and Marland answered that it would be difficult to simplify the process that far, but the Office was attempting to consolidate its grant-making process into "simplified delivery of monies."

Parting Broadside

In a parting broadside Brademas noted the Commissioner's allusion to the Drug Abuse Education Program. He said:

> . . . You are aware that law was also written in this subcommittee, and I would be less than candid if I did not observe the Administration came before this Subcommittee and opposed the enactment of that

law, even as it opposed the enactment of the Environmental Education Act.

We passed those laws over your opposition, we appropriated money over your opposition, and we are now
trying to persuade you to carry out the law of the
land, hopefully, not over your opposition, and I think
as we have suggested, we made great progress this
morning, Dr. Marland. . . .

The hearings had produced a formal commitment from
the Executive Branch that there would be no further delays in carrying out the expressed intent of Congress. All
together, the three hearings had informed the Administration of the continuing high level of Congressional interest
in this program and had produced some dramatic results.
When the hearings ended there was an official Advisory
Council with a date set for its first meeting, and there was
the official promise that the Office of Environmental Education would be established within five weeks. In fact, a
press release from OE went out the next day announcing
the creation of the Office.

The three sets of hearings came so quickly that the Administration was caught off guard, and it simply did not
react fast enough to cover itself. In this instance Congress
had more flexibility and maneuverability—taking advantage of the timing—than often is possible for the more
efficient managerial model, the executive branch. Commissioner Marland made an admirable defense, but he
was stuck with a situation not entirely of his making, and
he had to ride it out, unpleasant as it sometimes became.

Through exercising its oversight function, Congress was
able to keep its hands on legislation it had passed one
year earlier and had committed to the uncertainties of

implementation by the Executive Branch. The first branch had seemingly done everything it could to give life to the legislative program it had envisioned, but the task was not over. After the first oversight hearings were concluded there was little doubt that more would follow. The stone of Sisyphus would probably never remain at the top of the hill.

CHAPTER

9

Epilogue

ON OCTOBER 29, 1971, one day after the Brademas oversight hearings, the Office of Environmental Education was officially designated. This event, together with the announcement the day before that the Advisory Council had been created, indicated that the Administration had officially established the management structure to carry out the purposes of the Act. The program was now firmly implanted on its statutory base within the Office of Education. The staff could carry out its duties of funding, visiting, and evaluating projects and providing technical assistance to other authorities within the Office of Education and to other federal agencies on environmental education activities with greater certainty about the future status of the program.

The first meeting of the Advisory Council was held on the weekend of December 3 through 5. On Friday evening, December 3, the Council members, coming from as far away as California and Puerto Rico, met at a dinner with members of the OEE staff, staff members from Congress who had been involved in the legislation, and Congressman Brademas. Other members of Congress were invited but were unable to attend.

Brademas spoke briefly after the meeting, emphasizing that the importance of the Council was to assist the office in formulating policy for the program and to keep the wheels of progress moving. He said that the Council, like Congress, was a public entity with the responsibility of overseeing the expenditures of public funds by the Executive Branch.

The Congressman also was happy to announce that on that very day the Senate had passed an amendment introduced by Senator Nelson to add $2.5 million to the $3.5 million already enacted into law for environmental education. The action came on the floor of the Senate during debate over a supplemental-appropriations bill. If approved in the House–Senate conference, the total appropriation for FY 1972 would be $6 million, marking for the second time in one year a congressionally inspired increase in funding for the program. The House conferees rejected the amendment, however, and no additional funds were appropriated for that year. A major reason for the failure of this amendment was that when an appropriations bill comes to the conference table, floor amendments have relatively little power to change funding levels (as contrasted with amendments acted upon at the time the bill is still in committee). The legislative history of the amendment consists of about 10 to 60 minutes of floor debate, and there is no hearing record backing up the request, as there was with the supplemental appropriation for environmental education the year before.

At appropriations conferences floor amendments are the

first to be discussed. Unless unusually strong pressure is exerted in favor of the amendment, the amount asked is usually greatly reduced or eliminated altogether. Nelson's initiative was not fruitful. Congress had already increased funding for the Act by 75 percent, and a 200-percent increase over that year's budget request, without a strong and favorable legislative record, was found not to be justifiable in the conference.

When the President's budget for FY 1973 was sent to Congress on January 24, 1972, it contained a $3.18-million request for the environmental education program. Seemingly this was a decrease over the previous year's level of $3.5 million, but the amount was the same. This year the salaries and expenses to run the program were not to come out of the appropriation, as they had in the previous two years, but out of the Commissioner's general administrative fund. This was another sign that the program was maturing.

The program, however, was beset with administrative difficulties. On March 15 it was announced that the director of the Office of Environmental Education, Dr. Robert Gilkey, who had held the position for less than a year, was fired effective May 15, with the explanation that he did not have a solid enough environmental background. However, the firing may also have been related to a question over insubordination arising from testimony he had given before the Senate oversight hearings in the fall (see memorandum in Appendix 2, pertinent to this chapter and Chapter 8).

One month after the firing the Brademas subcommittee held a second set of oversight hearings on the Environmental Education Act. In these hearings, which took place on April 17, 1972, the theme of Congressional distrust of the Executive Branch was expressed in even harsher terms than in the earlier hearings. The Subcommittee Chairman unleashed a sharp attack on the Office of Education for what he felt was a consistent and deliberate attempt not to carry out the intent of Congress.

By this time Mr. Brademas did not believe much of what the Administration was saying, as is clearly evident in his questioning of Dr. Don Davies, the Director of the Office under which the Office of Environmental Education was placed, and Mrs. Ella Mae Turner, Chairman of the recently created Advisory Council.

Early in the testimony Brademas expressed his concern over what he saw as the larger issues involved. He said:

> ... There is an increasing concern on the part of members of Congress, both Democrats and Republicans, about the respect in the Executive Branch of government for carrying out the intent of Congress. It is not a question of doing Congress a favor. It is a question of obeying the law of the land.

He was disturbed when Gilkey did not appear, as requested, and he was not satisfied by Davies' answers as to Gilkey's absence. He asked, "What are you trying to hide down there?" Davies continued to explain that Gilkey was not an environmentalist and that it was thought important that a man with environmental qualities head the office. Brademas replied:

> Can you not read the English language down there? Don't you know what the purpose of the bill is? Why did you not appoint this kind of person in the first

place, if that was your understanding?
Did you read the hearings? Did you read the Committee report on the bill?

Davies responded, "Yes, sir."
Brademas continued to discuss the praise the Commissioner had expressed for Gilkey at the last hearings and
the commendations he received more recently. Then he
asked:

> Now, do you understand why we have a hard time
> trusting the integrity of the Administration of these
> programs? And you expect us to give you more au-
> thority under the renewal program.* You cannot even
> competently administer a modest program like this
> down there.

The Chairman's reference to the renewal program at this
particular point was a direct threat that if the Office of
Education did not follow congressional wishes in this case,
it might not expect his support on one of its own priority
efforts.

Asked what major problems he saw with respect to
achieving the program's goals, Davies listed three problem areas. First, he saw a need to build the intellectual

---

* The renewal program, an Administration initiative, was much larger
in scope than the Environmental Education Act and would consolidate
several programs to allow for a more comprehensive approach to supporting the needs of local school systems. The consolidation would also
eliminate a number of categorical programs, thus giving the Office of
Education more administrative flexibility and reducing the degree of its
accountability to Congress—a factor Congress was very suspicious of. The
renewal program was a precursor of the special revenue sharing program
for education proposed by the Administration in early 1973.

underpinnings of the concept of environmental education. He did not believe that the definition was sharp enough to be easily understood and communicated.

Second, Davies felt it was important to make progress on coordination and cooperation with other offices in the Office of Education. Over $11 million had been targeted from other funding authorities within the Office of Education for that current fiscal year. Davies indicated at the hearings that $4.6 million had already been earmarked for environmental education projects. The Office thus was to an extent doing what former Commissioner Allen had tried to get it to do at the beginning of environmental education efforts. While progress was being made, Davies indicated much would have to be accomplished before a definite pattern of operation and management, with respect to coordination, was established.

The third difficulty with the program was the need to solve certain management and administration problems within the office itself. This was in part due to the maverick style of the environmental education staff, which created inherent management difficulties.

The next witness was Ella Mae Turner, a black music teacher from the Watts section of Los Angeles who was Chairman of the Advisory Council. She discussed the activities of the Council since its creation. The Council had conducted two meetings in which it organized itself into a steering committee and four functional operating committees. It had developed and prepared bylaws, a code of ethics, a plan of visiting projects supported by the Act, and had submitted an annual report to the Commissioner shortly before the hearings.

Ms. Turner recommended, on behalf of the Council, that Congress provide full funding for the program, and that in order for "the Advisory Council to meet its statutory mandate from Congress as an oversight body, its budget also must be expanded above the current level."

Brademas questioned her about the primary functions assigned to the Council by the Act. First, he wanted to know if the Council had been involved in helping the Office of Education prepare the regulations for operation of programs under the Act. Second, he asked if the Council had participated in the allocation of its funds. To both of these questions the response was an unqualified no. He also asked if the Council had helped develop criteria to evaluate projects to be funded. The chairman said that some criteria were developed, but not at the instigation of the Office of Education.

Brademas then quoted from the Act to indicate how strongly he felt about these matters. He stated:

> "The Council shall," now I interrupt myself for a brief lesson in civics. When the Congress writes a law that says "shall," that means "must." You have to do it. It does not have the same meaning as "may," which means you can do it if you feel like it.

He continued:

> This is again . . . an instance of the clear violation by the United States Office of Education of the legislative mandate of the Congress. If you cannot read, then we will get a "right to read" program and a renewal strategy for the United States Office of Education. . . .

Davies replied that the guidelines for FT 1972 were prepared during the summer of 1971 and sent out to the field in October 1971, and that the Council was created in December 1971. The Chairman saw this reverse sequence as the fault of the Office of Education.

Davies said that the development of regulations regarding operation of the overall program was currently in the initial stages, and that if the Council members had not yet seen them, they would do so immediately. He was pressed on this and admitted that he had not known the Council did not see the regulations. He blamed the problem on not being properly notified by his staff.

Brademas' reply expressed his basic concern over the question of competency or integrity as related to carrying out the Environmental Education Act. He said:

> It is not a question of competence; it is a question of integrity. You [the Office of Education] just don't bother to pay attention to what the Congress writes in the law of the land.

The Chairman felt that if the Office of Education was competent, there should have been no major confrontations over the Act. Because there were such confrontations, and assuming the competency of the Office, he could only challenge its integrity. Brademas said later in an interview that his experience with this Act deepened his distrust of the intentions of the Executive Branch and brought out to him more clearly the importance of the oversight function as a means of strengthening the congressional role in the formulation of national policy and of maintaining a viable system of checks and balances between the first and second branches of government.

On this note the history of the Environmental Education Act, for the purposes of this book, ended. However, the fate of the Act is uncertain after June 30, 1974, when its authorization ends. The Administration intends then to discontinue the program and disband the Office of Environmental Education. The Congress wants to extend the Act for an additional three years. But that is another story.

FINAL COMMENT

The book portrays the congressional process by describing the history of the Environmental Education Act from the point of its beginnings as an idea in the form of a congressional initiative until it became a reality—an operational program with a statutory base. Translating the concept of environmental education into a national policy and an ongoing activity in the Office of Education was accomplished in a step-by-step movement through the legislative, appropriations, and oversight phases of congressional operation. This movement demonstrated the interrelatedness of these three functions and the resulting interaction between the legislative and executive branches. The importance of these relationships and tensions is pointed out throughout the book, particularly where they exemplify the fundamental political doctrines of separation of powers and checks and balances. The dynamics of the process illustrate, at least from the congressional perspective, that politics is an art and not a science. The real and potential barriers and constraints that could hamper the progress of the bill had to be overcome through a sequence of actions that were taken largely as the situation dictated and were subject to a high degree of unpredictability.

The three major functions of Congress are interrelated

in that the success of the first, legislation, depends upon the other two, appropriations and oversight. Without the first supplemental appropriation, environmental education might not have been included as an item of consideration in the President's forthcoming budget. Without the over-sight hearings, the Executive Branch might not have officially created the organizational structure mandated by the Act. Although it is obvious that these congressional actions contributed to these events, it is not possible accurately to predict what would have happened without them.

The interaction between the two branches on the Environmental Education Act exemplified the endless debate over the concept of checks and balances. The Act was structured so that Congress would have a handle for maintaining better accountability over the implementation of the Act including the intent of Congress by the Executive Branch.

At the same time the Executive Branch can serve as a checking force against powerful thrusts of Congress. In the case of the Environmental Education Act the Executive Branch was legitimately concerned that legislation was being forced upon it beyond the intent of the Constitution, and Administration resistance to some extent slowed the progress of the bill. As a result further debate occurred between the branches over the issue, and the Administration had more opportunity to influence the formulation of national policy.

Closely paralleling the doctrine of checks and balances is the separation of powers concept. The history of the bill portrays the differing perspectives of the legislative and executive branches with regard to this basic premise undergirding a democratic society. The internal-structuring amendment to the Act, which mandated the creation of an Office of Environmental Education and provided for a director at a specific Civil Service level, was seen by the Executive Branch as an over stepping of the inherent powers of Congress. In this case both sides were acting within the perception of their institutional prerogatives, which are more real than the reality of that perceived.

Finally, even after Congress had followed through on its legislative initiatives, as epitomized in its exercise of the oversight function, the ultimate fate of the program within the federal bureaucracy remained uncertain. It was still unclear if the long journey from idea to reality was successful, or if the Environmental Education Act would eventually dissolve into oblivion.

Afterword

As Dennis W. Brezina and Allen Overmyer point out in their introduction, this is a book about Congress in action.

But it is more than that, for it is also the story of the transformation of a growing impulse to heal our ravaged environment into the beginnings of an effort, albeit modest, by the federal government to support the education of our people about the environment of which we are a part.

There have been many descriptions of the ways we have befouled our environment. Yet there have been few so eloquent as that given to my subcommittee by the distinguished contemporary American painter, Robert Motherwell, when we were considering the Environmental Education Act.

Said Mr. Motherwell:

> I suppose America began as a few people on a vast tract of land, so vast that one could be as greedy and wasteful as one wanted, and there was still more. That time is gone. Now there are millions of people and millions more in the offing, and the vast land is a park filled with waste—rusting cars, bottles, garbage, enormous signs seducing you to buy what you don't want or need, housing projects that don't show a rudi-

mentary sense of proportion in any shape or line or
material—suburbs that are a parody of the barrenness
of the Bronx and the gaudiness of Las Vegas.

Indeed, if God had said to a group of men, "Here is
a vast park of millions of square miles. Let's see how
quickly you can cover it with everything that is an
affront to the human spirit, and above all be certain
that it is done on a scale of such extravagance and
waste and lack of regard for the sensibilities of the
inhabitants of the other parks in the world," then we
might by definition call that group of men that God
so addressed Americans.

No wonder our youth are up in arms!

In recent years the Congress of the United States and
successive presidents have moved to respond to this
frontal assault on what Kenneth Boulding has called
"Spaceship Earth." Senators Edmund S. Muskie of Maine
and Gaylord Nelson of Wisconsin and many others in
Congress have helped write a series of measures aimed at
enhancing our capacity to protect the environment and
prevent its pollution.

Yet I believe—and I do not think that champions of
clean air, land, and water would disagree—that if we are
to gain the ability to make substantial progress in meeting
our ecological crisis, we are going to need a citizenry informed and educated about the whole spectrum of issues
called environmental; and we are going to require as well
changes in basic attitudes toward the environment and
man's place in it.

That is why on November 12, 1969, several colleagues
and I in the House of Representatives introduced the
Environmental Education Act, a bill to authorize Federal

funds to support elementary and secondary-school courses on ecology, as well as curriculum development and teacher training for environmental studies.

On October 30, 1970, President Nixon signed this measure into law—the product of 13 days of public hearings, several more "markup" sessions by the Select Education Subcommittee on the Education and Labor Committee of the House of Representatives, and of debate and voting in the House and Senate. Yet if the signing of the bill into law had been the end of the legislative process, I do not believe that the authors would have written *Congress in Action: The Environmental Education Act.* For the events that shaped the original proposal into a federal statute and the history of the Environmental Education Act since then afford a continuous demonstration of how our separation of powers system of government works.

Indeed, the authors here etch a classic picture of the tensions between the executive and legislative branches of our national government. For in addition to illustrating the actual operations of our federal government and focusing attention on a major issue, the environmental crisis, *Congress in Action* provides a revealing example of the extraordinary prescience of the men who framed the checks and balances of our Constitution almost 200 years ago.

Congress in Action contains particularly useful lessons for the citizen interested in how the federal government, especially the legislative branch, initiates and shapes policy.

For example, the chapter describing the societal background against which we in Congress began considering the Environmental Education Act stresses the need for modern men and women to develop genuine respect for their natural surroundings as well as explaining the role environmental education can play in encouraging that respect.

The chapter also demonstrates the importance of public opinion and the best scientific thinking in the formulation of social policy.

In a similar fashion, while many Americans are familiar with the hearings that Congress holds in considering legislative proposals to authorize certain activities, many people are not aware that the House and Senate Appropriations committees also conduct hearings to consider how much money should be made available to carry out the purposes of the authorizing legislation.

Nor are many citizens familiar with the function of legislative oversight, whereby Congress inquires into the effectiveness of the actions of the executive branch in implementing the laws Congress passes.

Since the last oversight hearings held by the Select Education Subcommittee on the Environmental Education Act in April 1972, a new Director of the Office of Environmental Education has been appointed and the Advisory Council mandated by the Act to play a key role in its operation has been approved.

But more important still to the future of the Environmental Education Act, which began with such promising support from both Democrats and Republicans in Congress, may be the attitude of the Administration of President Nixon.

For even as the Administration originally opposed passage of the Environmental Education Act, later fought adequate appropriations for it, and delayed both establishing the Office of Environmental Education and appointing the Advisory Council, as I write—on Earth

Day 1973—President Nixon has called for an end to this fledgling effort to help Americans understand the environmental dimension of 20-century life.

For the Administration's budget for fiscal year 1974 contains no money at all for environmental education and proposes to let the Environmental Education Act wither away. Many of us in Congress will seek to extend and improve the programs made possible by the Environmental Education Act in its first months of life.

But whatever the fate of the Environmental Education Act, the story of the shaping of this legislation must encourage concerned citizens everywhere to make a serious commitment to the search for greater knowledge and understanding of our environment.

If the authors' book can help build such commitment, it will have made a significant contribution to winning the environmental challenge.

JOHN BRADEMAS
Select Subcommittee on Education
House of Representatives
April 1973

1

The Environmental Education Act
(PL 91-516)

Public Law 91-516
91st Congress, H. R. 18260
October 30, 1970

An Act

To authorize the United States Commissioner of Education to establish education programs to encourage understanding of policies, and support of activities, designed to enhance environmental quality and maintain ecological balance.

Be it enacted by the Senate and House of Representatives of the United States of America in Congress assembled, That this Act may be cited as the "Environmental Education Act".

STATEMENT OF FINDINGS AND PURPOSE

SEC. 2. (a) The Congress of the United States finds that the deterioration of the quality of the Nation's environment and of its ecological balance poses a serious threat to the strength and vitality of the people of the Nation and is in part due to poor understanding of the Nation's environment and of the need for ecological balance; that presently there do not exist adequate resources for educating and informing citizens in these areas, and that concerted efforts in educating citizens about environmental quality and ecological balance are therefore necessary.

(b) It is the purpose of this Act to encourage and support the development of new and improved curricula to encourage understanding of policies, and support of activities designed to enhance environmental quality and maintain ecological balance; to demonstrate the use of such curricula in model educational programs and to evaluate the effectiveness thereof; to provide support for the initiation and maintenance of programs in environmental education at the elementary and secondary levels; to disseminate curricular materials and other information for use in educational programs throughout the Nation; to provide training programs for teachers, other educational personnel, public service personnel, and community, labor, and industrial and business leaders and employees, and government employees at State, Federal, and local levels; to provide for the planning of outdoor ecological study centers; to provide for community education programs on preserving and enhancing environmental quality and maintaining ecological balance; and to provide for the preparation and distribution of materials by mass media in dealing with the environment and ecology.

ENVIRONMENTAL EDUCATION

SEC. 3. (a) (1) There is established, within the Office of Education, an office of environmental education (referred to in this section as the "office") which, under the supervision of the Commissioner, through regulations promulgated by the Secretary, shall be responsible for (A) the administration of the program authorized by subsection (b) and (B) the coordination of activities of the Office of Education which are related to environmental education. The office shall be headed by a Director who shall be compensated at a rate not to exceed that prescribed for grade GS-17 in section 5332 of title 5, United States Code.

(2) For the purposes of this Act, the term "environmental education" means the educational process dealing with man's relationship with his natural and manmade surroundings, and includes the relation of population, pollution, resource allocation and depletion, conservation, transportation, technology, and urban and rural planning to the total human environment.

(b) (1) The Commissioner shall carry out a program of making grants to, and contracts with, institutions of higher education, State and local educational agencies, regional educational research organizations, and other public and private agencies, organizations, and institutions (including libraries and museums) to support research, demonstration, and pilot projects designed to educate the public on the problems of environmental quality and ecological balance, except that no grant may be made other than to a nonprofit agency, organization or institution.

(2) Funds appropriated for grants and contracts under this section shall be available for such activities as—

(A) the development of curricula (including interdisciplinary curricula) in the preservation and enhancement of environmental quality and ecological balance;

(B) dissemination of information relating to such curricula and to environmental education, generally;

(C) in the case of grants to State and local educational agencies, for the support of environmental education programs at the elementary and secondary education levels;

(D) preservice and inservice training programs and projects (including fellowship programs, institutes, workshops, symposiums, and seminars) for educational personnel to prepare them to teach in subject matter areas associated with environmental quality and ecology, and for public service personnel, government employees, and business, labor, and industrial leaders and employees;

(E) planning of outdoor ecological study centers;

(F) community education programs on environmental quality, including special programs for adults; and

(G) preparation and distribution of materials suitable for use by the mass media in dealing with the environment and ecology.

In addition to the activities specified in the first sentence of this paragraph, such funds may be used for projects designed to demon-

strate, test, and evaluate the effectiveness of any such activities,
whether or not assisted under this section.

(3)(A) Financial assistance under this subsection may be made
available only upon application to the Commissioner. Applications
under this subsection shall be submitted at such time, in such form,
and containing such information as the Secretary shall prescribe by
regulation and shall be approved only if it—

(i) provides that the activities and services for which assistance is sought will be administered by, or under the supervision
of, the applicant;

(ii) describes a program for carrying out one or more of the
purposes set forth in the first sentence of paragraph (2) which
holds promise of making a substantial contribution toward at-
taining the purposes of this section;

(iii) sets forth such policies and procedures as will insure
adequate evaluation of the activities intended to be carried out
under the application;

(iv) sets forth policies and procedures which assure that Federal funds made available under this Act for any fiscal year will
be so used as to supplement and, to the extent practical, increase
the level of funds that would, in the absence of such Federal
funds, be made available by the applicant for the purposes described in section 3, and in no case supplant such funds.

(v) provides for such fiscal control and fund accounting procedures as may be necessary to assure proper disbursement of
and accounting for Federal funds paid to the applicant under
this title; and

(vi) provides for making an annual report and such other
reports, in such form and containing such information, as the
Commissioner may reasonably require and for keeping such
records, and for affording such access thereto as the Commissioner
may find necessary to assure the correctness and verification of
such reports.

(B) Applications from local educational agencies for financial
assistance under this Act may be approved by the Commissioner only
if the State educational agency has been notified of the application
and been given the opportunity to offer recommendations.

(C) Amendments of applications shall, except as the Secretary
may otherwise provide by or pursuant to regulation, be subject to
approval in the same manner as original applications.

(4) Federal assistance to any program or project under this section,
other than those involving curriculum development, dissemination of
curricular materials, and evaluation, shall not exceed 80 per centum of
the cost of such program for the first fiscal year of its operation,
including costs of administration, unless the Commissioner deter-
mines, pursuant to regulations adopted and promulgated by the Secretary establishing objective criteria for such determinations, that
assistance in excess of such percentages is required in furtherance of

the purposes of this section. The Federal share for the second year shall not exceed 60 per centum, and for the third year 40 per centum. Non-Federal contributions may be in cash or kind, fairly evaluated, including but not limited to plant, equipment, and services.

(c)(1) There is hereby established an Advisory Council on Environmental Education consisting of twenty-one members appointed by the Secretary. The Secretary shall appoint one member as Chairman. The Council shall consist of persons appointed from the public and private sector with due regard to their fitness, knowledge, and experience in matters of, but not limited to, academic, scientific, medical, legal, resource conservation and production, urban and regional planning, and information media activities as they relate to our society and affect our environment, and shall give due consideration to geographical representation in the appointment of such members: *Provided, however,* That the Council shall consist of not less than three ecologists and three students.

(2) The Council shall—

(A) advise the Commissioner and the office concerning the administration of, preparation of general regulations for, and operation of programs assisted under this section;

(B) make recommendations to the office with respect to the allocation of funds appropriated pursuant to subsection (d) among the purposes set forth in paragraph (2) of subsection (b) and the criteria to be used in approving applications, which criteria shall insure an appropriate geographical distribution of approved programs and projects throughout the Nation;

(C) develop criteria for the review of applications and their disposition; and

(D) evaluate programs and projects assisted under this section and disseminate the results thereof.

TECHNICAL ASSISTANCE

SEC. 4. The Secretary of Health, Education, and Welfare, in cooperation with the heads of other agencies with relevant jurisdiction, shall, insofar as practicable upon request, render technical assistance to local educational agencies, public and private nonprofit organizations, institutions of higher education, agencies of local, State, and Federal governments and other agencies deemed by the Secretary to play a role in preserving and enhancing environmental quality and maintaining ecological balance. The technical assistance shall be designed to enable the recipient agency to carry on education programs which are related to environmental quality and ecological balance.

SMALL GRANTS

SEC. 5. (a) In addition to the grants authorized under section 3, the Commissioner, from the sums appropriated, shall have the authority to make grants, in sums not to exceed $10,000 annually, to nonprofit organizations such as citizens groups, volunteer organizations working in the environmental field, and other public and private non-profit agencies, institutions, or organizations for conducting courses, workshops, seminars, symposiums, institutes, and conferences, especially for adults and community groups (other than the group funded).

(b) Priority shall be given to those proposals demonstrating innovative approaches to environmental education.

(c) For the purposes of this section, the Commissioner shall require evidence that the interested organization or group shall have been in existence one year prior to the submission of a proposal for Federal funds and that it shall submit an annual report on Federal funds expended.

(d) Proposals submitted by organizations and groups under this section shall be limited to the essential information required to evaluate them, unless the organization or group shall volunteer additional information.

ADMINISTRATION

SEC. 6. In administering the provisions of this Act, the Commissioner is authorized to utilize the services and facilities of any agency of the Federal Government and of any other public or private agency or institution in accordance with appropriate agreements, and to pay for such services either in advance or by way of reimbursement, as may be agreed upon. The Commissioner shall publish annually a list and description of projects supported under this Act and shall distribute such list and description to interested educational institutions, citizens' groups, conservation organizations, and other organizations and individuals involved in enhancing environmental quality and maintaining ecological balance.

AUTHORIZATION

SEC. 7. There is authorized to be appropriated $5,000,000 for the fiscal year ending June 30, 1971, $15,000,000 for the fiscal year ending June 30, 1972, and $25,000,000 for the fiscal year ending June 30, 1973, for carrying out the purposes of this Act.

Approved October 30, 1970.

LEGISLATIVE HISTORY:

HOUSE REPORT No. 91-1362 (Comm. on Education and Labor).
SENATE REPORT No. 91-1164 (Comm. on Labor and Public Welfare).
CONGRESSIONAL RECORD, Vol. 116 (1970):
    Aug. 3, considered and passed House.
    Sept. 21, considered and passed Senate, amended.
    Oct. 13, House concurred in Senate amendments with an amend-
        ment; Senate concurred in House amendment.

2

The Memo of Commissioner Marland

COMMISSIONER MARLAND was furious when he learned about the testimony Dr. Gilkey had given before the first set of Senate oversight hearings (Senate Subcommittee on Intergovernmental Relations) on the Administration's handling of the Environmental Education Act. On October 26 the Commissioner wrote a memorandum to Dr. Rodney H. Brady, Assistant Secretary of HEW for Administration and Management, with whom Gilkey had appeared at those hearings, detailing the "correct" manner in which Gilkey should have answered the questions. He singled out Gilkey's responses about no office being created, his having no authority to administer the program, the number of times he had called on the Commissioner, and the legality of making grants with no Advisory Council in existence. The Commissioner contended that Gilkey had "behaved either in ignorance of the facts for which he should be held responsible for knowing; or at worst he was consciously insubordinate."

October 26, 1971

MEMORANDUM FOR HONORABLE RODNEY H. BRADY

Since joining the Office of Education nearly a year ago, I have at no time been as furious as I am this weekend, upon reading the hearing transcript enclosed with your letter of October 18. I am writing this at home, to give you the full flavor of my outrage, realizing that in so doing I am shooting from the hip. A copy of this letter will go to Dr. Robert Gilkey. If he is able to reconcile my judgment of his testimony I shall ask you to return this letter without action. If, in the major categories of his testimony, he is not able to explain his position, this letter will be entered in his file, as the least of the actions I am weighing.

I have read your testimony of October 8 with care. It is accurate. You apparently were accompanied by Dr. Gilkey to this hearing as a backup for technical assistance. As nearly as I can judge, he behaved either in ignorance of the facts for which he should be held responsible for knowing, or at worst he was consciously insubordinate.

I shall turn to Dr. Gilkey's testimony and offer my own responses, as I believe the truth to be, in juxtaposition with his:

Page 907 (starting at Line 20)

Mr. Turner.   Dr. Gilkey, ... do you report to him (the Commissioner)?

Dr. Gilkey.   Not on an administrative basis. We report to Dr. Davies who is Associate Commissioner for Development.

Correct Answer.   Our organization provides for high priority programs to be centered close to the Commissioner under Dr. Davies, Deputy Commissioner for Development.

* * * * * *

Mr. Turner.   He is what?

Dr. Gilkey.   Associate Commissioner for Development.

Correct Answer.   Deputy Commissioner for Development, that office charged under our management system with the breakthrough, innovative thrusts of the Office, along with Right to Read, Drug Abuse Education, Teacher Reform, etc.

* * * * * *

Mr. Turner.   Who does Dr. Davies report to?

Dr. Gilkey.   To the Commissioner.

Correct Answer.   For management purposes, and general administrative structure, Dr. Davies reports to the Commissioner. Program officers, such as I, especially in high priority programs such as Environmental Education, have direct access to the Commissioner. He has stated this many times.

* * * * * *

Mr. Turner. But you don't have an office? It is not like the Office of Higher Education?

Dr. Gilkey. No, it is currently a program, I believe, on an informal basis. It has not been officially so designated but our previous reporting position was to the Director of the Office of Priority Management and at that time he designated us as a program and since that time we have still gone on in that situation.

Correct Answer. Up until recently the Commissioner placed all high priority programs, such as mine, in the Office of Priority Management. We do indeed have an office, a good staff, and adequate facilities, even though we need more of both. The reason for the Office of Priority Management was that newly created organizations, such as mine, with no staff, no director, no funds, needed an initial seed-bed to get started. That seed-bed period is now concluded, and we have been given full status under the Deputy Commissioner for Development as a fully established component of the Office of Education. (An Administrative Announcement placing us in this position was released on August 12, 1971.) This placed our program in as high a position as any program in the Office in terms of the organizational hierarchy. Dr. Davies is in contact with the Commissioner daily.

* * * * * *

Mr. Turner. Do you have line authority to coordinate the activities of the Office of Education which are related to environmental education?

Dr. Gilkey. No.

Correct Answer. I am the director of the Environmental Education program. As such I have administered the total activities relating to Environmental Education in the Office since coming aboard in June, about four months ago. I am the principal agent of the Office in this field, not only for the $3 million appropriation over which I have complete charge, but for some $11 million in cooperative programs from other parts of the Office, for which I have a coordinating responsibility, under direct orders from the Commissioner, with the administrators of those programs. In brief, yes.

Mr. Turner. You do not have that?

Dr. Gilkey. No.

Correct Answer. Yes.

Mr. Turner. And the law so states you should. Are you the head of an Office of Environmental Education?

Dr. Gilkey. No, sir.

Correct Answer. Yes, sir. While my papers may still be in process, I am performing the duties.

Mr. Turner. And the law so states you should be. Are you compensated at a rate of GS-17?

Dr. Gilkey. No, sir.

Correct Answer. Mr. Turner, this is a $3 million program. You asked earlier about our comparison with the Bureau of Higher Education. That is a $1.7 billion program. The Office of Education, historically, and in spite of the Commissioner's intensive efforts, remains fairly low in comparative scale of supergrades with other reform agencies, probably because it has been in business for over a hundred years. A GS-17 rating for a $3 million program, with a staff of 10-12, would create totally inconsistent administrative patterns, and would doubtless be very difficult to defend in Civil Service protocols. We have GS–15s and 16s administrating programs at the level of a billion dollars and half-billion dollars, with national priorities of a level of urgency equal even to Environmental Education, such as the disadvantaged, integration and student aid. A GS–17 in my office, much as I would enjoy it, personally, would be completely incongruous with present OE organization. The language of the Act authorizes "up to GS–17"; It does not mandate it.

Mr. Turner.   How many times have you been in the Office of the Commissioner of Education in the last two weeks?

Dr. Gilkey.   The last two weeks? Not once. The Commissioner has been away.

Correct Answer.   Not specifically in the last two weeks. I have been trying to find time to get there. The Commissioner called me in at a time convenient to me two or three weeks ago.

(Note: The Commissioner was away for one week in mid-September at a UNESCO meeting in Geneva which dealt in part with Environmental Education. Otherwise he has been available to any staff request for calendar time, and certainly in two weeks preceding this October 8 hearing.)

Mr. Turner.   How many in the last month?

Dr. Gilkey.   Not once.

Correct Answer.   Again, I have been invited by the Commissioner to see him, but I have been awaiting the completion of major current activities in order to give him a full accounting of our progress at the time I see him.

Mr. Turner.   How many in the last two months?

Dr. Gilkey.   Not once.

Correct Answer.   You should know, Mr. Turner, that while I may
not have visited the Commissioner's Office recently, he has visited my office on at least two
occasions. He took a very active interest in our
record-breaking day-night-weekend operation,
which he demanded, to process our grants to
project applicants in less than ten days. He in-
terrogated not only the select scientists that we
had assembled as proposal evaluators, but the
students and young people we had assembled, to
ascertain the procedures and criteria on grant
awards. When the Commissioner comes to my
office I don't feel I have a necessity to recipro-
cate with a visit to his.

Mr. Turner.   How many in the last six months?

Dr. Gilkey.   Once, I believe.

Correct Answer.   Mr. Turner, I have only been in the Office of
Education for four months. I understand that a
lengthy national search for a Director, in which
Dr. Marland participated personally, sought to
discover the right leader who would be not only
a first-rate ecologist, but a manager and administrator familiar and skilled in government. After
an exhaustive search, Dr. Marland found that he
could not in a reasonable period of time find this
combination. He therefore chose the compromise of naming me as Director, with a background of management, administrative and government-wide experience, including familiarity
with Congress, on the understanding that we
would draw heavily upon the scientific talent in
the Nation for backup, in staff, in consultant

services, and in the expertise of the National Advisory Committee. Dr. Marland personally chose me for this work, after lengthy conversations with top staff, and with him, and instructed me in my role as Director.

* * * * * *

Page 913 (starting at Line 19)

Following extensive reference by Mr. Turner to language pertaining to the role of the National Advisory Council, Mr. Turner asked whether the Secretary knew of grants being disbursed without the completion of the Advisory Council.

Dr. Brady.   I cannot answer that question specifically because I do not have that information with me.

Mr. Turner.   I understand that. Maybe Mr. Gilkey can.

Dr. Gilkey.   I cannot answer the question.

Senator Metcalf.   (Further exposition of the necessary role of the Advisory Council and exchanges with Dr. Brady, who should have been able to depend upon Dr. Gilkey's knowledge of the facts.)

Mr. Turner.   ... information has come to this Committee that the General Counsel of the Office of Education advised Commissioner Marland that he was skirting the law, skirting the law by handing out the grants without having the Advisory Council review them.

Do you know anthing about that, Mr. Gilkey?

Dr. Gilkey.   I am aware of the advice. I came in about the time we were giving the grants last June.

Correct Answer.   I do not know whether the Commissioner was aware of the caution on skirting the law or not. (Note: He was not.)

As soon as our Advisory Council is in place, during the next few weeks, it will of course be very much involved in our work. However, Mr. Chairman, Senator Metcalf, Mr. Turner, you should know of the circumstances under which Dr. Marland made the decision to proceed without delay with the administration of grants. The legislation had been anticipated by many potential grant recipients, and much publicity. It was passed on October 30, 1970, and we had the appropriation. Great interest and concern prevailed not only on the part of Dr. Marland to get the grants out, but equal interest and concern came from the field and from Congress.

It was clear that, based on experience, months could pass before the whole Advisory Council could be put into place and become operational. In spite of our best efforts, the interviewing, selection, balancing for race, geography, sex, professional competencies, the securing of acceptances, is a very labored and slow procedure if the membership is to be truly distinguished. The ultimate processing through channels for appointment alone, with hundreds of other similar committees, is extremely slow.

Therefore, it was clear to the Commissioner last June that we would not be likely to have an Advisory Council in place and functioning before late fall, long after the academic year had started. He established, in its stead, a provisional, ad hoc group of scientists, generalists, environmentalists, and young people to serve as the reviewing authority pending the formal appointment of the Advisory Council. This permitted us to make the grants on schedule for implementation in time to be effective this academic year rather than lose a year. The ad hoc advisors notably helped formulate the administrative policies. They actually reviewed and recommended approval or disapproval of proposals. We accepted these recommendations at virtually the 100% level. I know of no grant made, out of almost 2000 that we processed that did not have the endorsement of the ad hoc committee. Out of almost two thousand proposals we finally awarded 74 grants.

And now, Mr. Chairman, I should like to submit this accounting of our grant work so far. This is a popularized version of our formal report on environmental education activities so far this year. It was developed at the express direction of the Commissioner. It is intended for wide circulation to encourage lively participation by the education community in partnership with scientists and concerned citizens of all ages.

* * * * * *

That, Rod, is my reason for outrage. I am pondering whether to send this to the Congressmen at the hearing who clearly had reason for outrage themselves in light of this incompetent testimony, and I ask your advice on this matter.

I shall report to you the outcome of my forthcoming conversation on this subject with Dr. Gilkey.

I am grateful for your October 18 memo, and for your counsel.

S. P. Marland, Jr.
U.S. Commissioner of Education

cc: Dr. Don Davies
Dr. Robt. Gilkey
Dr. Chas. Saunders

3

Chronology of Environmental Education Act

Summer 1969	Office of Education student task force studies environmental education.
November 12, 1969	Environmental Education Act introduced in the House of Representatives by John Brademas (D–Ind.).
November 19, 1969	Environmental Education Act introduced in the Senate by Gaylord Nelson (D–Wis.).
December 11, 1969	Environmental Reclamation Education Act introduced in the Senate by Charles Goodell (R–N.Y.).
December 12, 1969	Commissioner of Education James Allen indicates in a memo to his staff that he is interested in making environmental education a priority item.
January 23, 1970	Commissioner Allen speaks on environmental education at a meeting of the American Council on Learned Societies.
February 9, 1970	Commissioner Allen creates the Task Force on Environmental/Ecological Education within OE.

March 24 through May 2, 1970	House Select Subcommittee on Education holds 13 days of hearings on Environmental Education Act.
April 21, 1970	Commissioner Allen testifies against the Environmental Education Act at the House hearings; his testimony is questioned that evening after his speech at the University of Wisconsin Earth Day activities.
April 22, 1970	Earth Day.
May 6, 1970	Senator Claiborne Pell (D–R.I.) introduces internal-structuring amendment to Environmental Education Act.
May 19 and 20, 1970	Senate Subcommittee on Education holds hearings on Environmental Education Act; Commissioner Allen announces Administration support of the Act.
June 12, 1970	Commissioner Allen resigns from his position at the request of the President as a result of his criticism of the Cambodian invasion.
June 24, 1970	House Subcommittee reports Environmental Education Act to full Education and Labor Committee.
July 30, 1970	Senate Subcommittee reports Environmental Education Act to full Labor and Public Welfare Committee.
July 31, 1970	House Committee on Education and Labor reports Environmental Education Act to House.
August 3, 1970	Environmental Education Act debated and passed by House of Representatives—289 yeas to 28 nays.
September 9, 1970	Senate Committee on Labor and Public Welfare reports Environmental Education Act to Senate.
September 21, 1970	Senate passes Environmental Education Act—64 yeas to 0 nays.
October 5, 1970	Compromise version of Environmental Education Act clears "mini-conference"; ready for final congressional action.

October 13, 1970 Conference version of Environmental Education Act passes House and Senate unanimously.

October 30, 1970 President Nixon signs Environmental Education Act into law (PL 91-516).

November 20, 1970 Nelson writes to Senator Byrd (D–W. Va.) requesting funding for Environmental Education Act in the supplemental appropriations bill for FY 1971.

December 4, 1970 Nelson appears before the Byrd Subcommittee to request funding for Environmental Education Act.

December 10, 1970 Sidney P. Marland, Jr., is confirmed by the Senate for the position of Commissioner of Education, replacing James Allen.

December 14, 1970 Senate passes supplemental-appropriations bill containing $2 million for environmental education in FY 1971.

December 22, 1970 Conference version of supplemental-appropriations bill passes Congress containing $2 million for environmental education.

January 8, 1971 President Nixon signs supplemental-appropriations bill with $2 million for environmental education.

January 29, 1971 Administration's FY 1972 budget presented to Congress with request for $2 million for environmental education.

April 7, 1971 House passes FY 1972 appropriations for OE with $2 million for environmental education.

April 15, 1971 Guidelines for applications for $2 million (FY 1971 funds) published by Office of Education.

May 15, 1971 Dr. Robert Gilkey hired to head environmental education program within OE.

May 24, 1971 Nelson writes to Senator Magnuson (D–Wash.) of Appropriations Committee requesting $15 million for environmental education in FY 1972.

May 26, 1971 Office of Education has received 1,925 pro-

	posals requesting grants from the $2 million appropriated for FY 1971 for environmental education.
June 10, 1971	Senate passes appropriations for OE with $5 million for environmental education in FY 1972.
June 30, 1971	74 projects receive funding in environmental education from the $2 million appropriated for FY 1971.
June 30, 1971	Congress passes the OE appropriations bill for FY 1972, which contains $3.5 million for environmental education.
October 8, 1971	Senate Subcommittee on Intergovernmental Relations holds oversight hearings on Environmental Education Act as part of its investigation into federal advisory councils.
October 14, 1971	Senate Subcommittee on Human Resources holds oversight hearings on the population-education aspects of the Environmental Education Act.
October 28, 1971	House Subcommittee on Education holds oversight hearings on progress of environmental education in the Office of Education.
October 28, 1971	Appointment of Advisory Council on Environmental Education announced by Commissioner Marland at House hearings.
October 29, 1971	Formation of Office of Environmental Education announced by Office of Education.
December 3, 1971	Nelson amendment to Senate supplemental-appropriations bill passes to increase funds for environmental education in FY 1972 by $2.5 million.
December 3, 1971	First meeting of the Advisory Council on Environmental Education held in Washington, D.C.
December 10, 1971	Conference version of the supplemental appropriations for FY 1972 passes Congress without additional funding for environmental education.

January 24, 1972   President's budget for FY 1973 includes $3.18 million for environmental education.

March 15, 1972   Office of Education announces firing of Dr. Robert Gilkey as Director of the Office of Environmental Education.

April 17, 1972   House Subcommittee on Education holds second set of oversight hearings on Environmental Education Act.

April 1972   More of the same. The nature of the conflict
to present   has not changed.

Index